SECURING RELIGIOUS LIBERTY

SECURING RELIGIOUS LIBERTY

*Principles for
Judicial Interpretation of the
Religion Clauses*

....

Jesse H. Choper

*The
University
of
Chicago
Press*

....

CHICAGO AND LONDON

JESSE H. CHOPER is the Earl Warren Professor of Public Law
at the University of California, Berkeley. His earlier
book, *Judicial Review and the National Political Process,*
winner of the Order of the Coif Triennial Book Award, is
also published by the University of Chicago Press.

The University of Chicago Press, Chicago 60637
The University of Chicago Press, Ltd., London
© 1995 by The University of Chicago
All rights reserved. Published 1995
Printed in the United States of America

04 03 02 01 00 99 98 97 96 95   1 2 3 4 5

ISBN: 0-226-10445-1 (cloth)

Library of Congress Cataloging-in-Publication Data

Choper, Jesse H.
Securing religious liberty : principles for judicial
interpretation of the religion clauses / Jesse H. Choper.
     p.   cm.
Includes index.
1. Freedom of religion—United States. 2. Church and state—
United States. 3. Judicial review—United States. I. Title.
KF4783.C47   1995
342.73′0852—dc20
[347.302852]   94-36239
                                                      CIP

This book is printed on acid-free paper.

TO MY SONS,

Marc Steven and Edward Nathaniel Choper

CONTENTS

Preface: A Personal Note

The first experience I can recall involving the separation of church and state arose when I was in seventh grade. At the beginning of each day at the public school I attended, all students gathered in the auditorium for "chapel." The session usually consisted of a series of announcements by the principal, sometimes followed by a brief program—for example, a pep talk by the football coach on the day before the game. The assembly always began with a teacher or administrator reading from the Bible, and all the students then recited the Lord's Prayer. This practice was contrary to my religious training and beliefs, and I responded in a variety of ways. Sometimes I remained silent throughout. Other times I repeated most of the prayer but stopped before the final line, as I saw my Roman Catholic friends do. Occasionally I participated fully in the prayer ceremony, though I often assuaged my guilt feelings by garbling some of the words. In any event, twelve years later when my law school course in Constitutional Law considered the materials on freedom of religion, these earlier personal recollections clearly generated a special interest on my part and unquestionably influenced my thinking about how the Religion Clauses should be interpreted.

As fate would have it, a substantial part of my clerkship with Chief Justice Earl Warren the next year was spent dealing with church-state issues. A relatively short time was devoted to reviewing the papers in *Torcaso v. Watkins*,[1] but the

---

1. 367 U.S. 488 (1961) (state requirement of belief in God as a test for public office violates the Religion Clauses).

Sunday Closing Law Cases[2] involved a major commitment. My initial reaction was that these state regulations violated both of the Religion Clauses. Further reflection, however (powerfully influenced by my law school training to search for "neutral principles" for the judicial resolution of legal problems and by my own evolving belief that this was especially important in respect to constitutional adjudication), eventually caused me to come to the opposite conclusion.

This sustained intellectual labor on the subject led naturally to my decision the following year to write my "tenure article" in the church-state area,[3] and during the next three decades the topic occupied the largest part of my scholarly agenda. This book draws heavily on my previous articles,[4] reevaluating their ideas and placing the issues in the context of a newly structured set of principles for judging the constitutionality of government action under the Religion Clauses of the First Amendment. Although mainly devoted to a substantive analysis of these constitutional provisions, the discus-

2. McGowan v. Maryland, 366 U.S. 420 (1961); Gallagher v. Crown Kosher Super Market, 366 U.S. 617 (1961); Two Guys from Harrison-Allentown, Inc. v. McGinley, 366 U.S. 582 (1961); Braunfeld v. Brown, 366 U.S. 599 (1961).

3. Religion in the Public Schools: A Proposed Constitutional Standard, 47 Minn. L. Rev. 329 (1963).

4. The Establishment Clause and Aid to Parochial Schools, 56 Calif. L. Rev. 260 (1968); The Religion Clauses of the First Amendment: Reconciling the Conflict, 41 U. Pitt. L. Rev. 673 (1980); Defining "Religion" in the First Amendment, 1982 U. Ill. L. Rev. 579; The Free Exercise Clause: A Structural Overview and an Appraisal of Recent Developments, 27 Wm. & Mary L. Rev. 943 (1986); Separation of Church and Stage, in Encyclopedia of the American Constitution 1650–59 (Leonard W. Levy & Kenneth L. Karst eds. 1986); The Establishment Clause and Aid to Parochial Schools—An Update, 75 Calif. L. Rev. 5 (1987); Church, State and the Supreme Court: Current Controversy, 29 Ariz. L. Rev. 551 (1987); The Establishment and the Free Exercise Clauses: Resolving the Inherent Tension, in The Constitutional Bases of Political and Social Change in the United States 73–94 (Shlomo Slonim ed. 1990); The Rise and Decline of the Constitutional Protection of Religious Liberty, 70 Neb. L. Rev. 651 (1991); Government Aid to Religious Institutions, in Encyclopedia of the American Constitution Supplement I 237–38 (1992); Separation of Church and State: "New" Directions by the "New" Supreme Court, 34 J. Church & State 363 (1992); Religion and Race under the Constitution: Similarities and Differences, 79 Cornell L. Rev. 491 (1994).

sion inevitably reflects my more general philosophy on the role of courts and judicial review.

I wish to express deep appreciation to several people who carefully reviewed the manuscript and made many helpful suggestions: two distinguished scholars in the church-state field—Douglas Laycock of the University of Texas School of Law and John H. Mansfield of Harvard Law School; my two Constitutional Law colleagues at Berkeley—Paul J. Mishkin and Robert C. Post; and two younger members of the Boalt Hall faculty who do not toil in this particular vineyard but whose comments were especially insightful—Einer R. Elhauge and Eric Rakowski. I should emphasize that none of them agrees with all, or even most of my approach, and that they all must be absolved of responsibility for any errors of fact, analysis, or judgment that persist. Thanks also go to my secretary, Theresa Wong, for her superb efforts in preparing the typescript, to Cathe Cashman for making the final revision, and to Ted Mermin of the class of 1996 for cheerfully and meticulously reviewing the manuscript and checking all citations.

A substantial part of the book was drafted when I was a scholar-in-residence at the Rockefeller Foundation's Bellagio Study and Conference Center at Lake Como, Italy. Everything at the Villa Serbelloni—the incomparably beautiful physical setting and surroundings, the wonderfully planned and executed amenities, the uninterrupted time to think and write, the exciting company of my fellow residents, and the extraordinary assistance of the entire staff—made it an experience very hard to match and one for which I am extremely grateful.

Last, but certainly not least, I most happily and obligingly acknowledge the continued encouragement of three dear friends—Sanford H. Kadish, Michael E. Smith, and Jan Vetter—who insisted that there could be a scholarly life for me after deanship.

1

Basic Postulates
and Alternative Theories

This book articulates a comprehensive thesis for adjudication of all significant issues that arise under the Religion Clauses , of the Constitution, which forbid laws "respecting an establishment of religion, or prohibiting the free exercise thereof." This effort requires reasoned elaboration of a set of principles that are grounded in the history and text of the First Amendment but that also take into account the values and traditions we have derived over time from the intentions of the framers and the language of the document. These principles should provide judges with intelligible guidelines for the exercise of discretion and judgment that inheres in constitutional decision making and should be designed to limit, as much as practicable, the intuitive tendency of these judges, acting in good faith, to bring their personal predilections to bear on the issues that come before them. This unavoidable infusion of individual biases not only conflicts with basic precepts of our democratic political system but also undermines fundamental values of personal liberty protected by the First Amendment. The cabining principles should also be capable of consistent application to the relevant problems while minimizing the inescapable number of disagreeable results.

PRELIMINARY CONSIDERATIONS

USE OF HISTORY IN CONSTITUTIONAL EXEGESIS

It is not my purpose to determine the proper weight that should be given in constitutional interpretation to such critical factors as text, original intent, constitutional structure, and contemporary values. Nonetheless, I should make several preliminary observations about the role of history.

It has been said that "[n]o provision of the Constitution is more closely tied to or given content by its generating history than the religious clause of the First Amendment."[1] Still, "[a] too literal quest for the advice of the Founding Fathers [would be] futile and misdirected."[2] First, there is a genuine question of "who should count as framers":[3] the members of the First Congress who proposed the Bill of Rights, the people who voted approval in the state ratification process, or perhaps even "the parties to the constitutional compact—[i.e.,] the states as political entities."[4] Moreover, actual government practices undertaken contemporaneously with or soon after the adoption of the Religion Clauses may be viewed, even more than words or thoughts, as providing especially clear insight into the contemplation of the founders.[5] Indeed, since most cases invoking the Religion Clauses involve state and local action rather than action by the national government, it may well be that the relevant inquiry concerns the history of the Fourteenth Amendment,[6] which has been construed to make the First Amendment's religion provisions applicable to the states.

Second, there is overwhelming difficulty in ascertaining the intentions of all those persons who were framers or rati-

1. Everson v. Board of Education, 330 U.S. 1, 33 (1947) (Rutledge, J., dissenting).
2. Abington School District v. Schempp, 374 U.S. 203, 237 (1963) (Brennan, J., concurring).
3. Charles Fried, Order and Law 62–63 (1991).
4. H. Jefferson Powell, The Original Understanding of Original Intent, 98 Harv. L. Rev. 885, 888 (1985).
5. See Wallace v. Jaffree, 472 U.S. 38, 100–106 (1985) (Rehnquist, J., dissenting). Contra, Rebecca L. Brown, Tradition and Insight, 103 Yale L.J. 177, 183–91 (1993); Douglas Laycock, "Noncoercive" Support for Religion: Another False Claim about the Establishment Clause, 26 Val. L. Rev. 37, 48–50 (1991).
6. See Steven G. Gey, Why Is Religion Special? Reconsidering the Accommodation of Religion under the Religion Clauses of the First Amendment, 52 U. Pitt. L. Rev. 75, 122 (1990).

fiers, either their attitudes about specific issues or, more generally, their broader design for how the Constitution should be interpreted over time in light of changed conditions and evolving values.[7] "Neither the Senate nor the House of Representatives kept official records of the debates over the Bill of Rights. There are only sketchy (and perhaps unreliable) unofficial reports of the House debate, and no unofficial reports whatsoever of the Senate's secret sessions. Records of the state legislatures that ratified the amendments are also nonexistent."[8] Moreover, some of the most important figures expressed changed (and even conflicting) views at varied times, in different forums, or to distinct audiences.[9]

Third, the specific historical record, rather than disclosing a coherent "intent of the framers" who most actively participated in the development of the Religion Clauses, suggests that those who primarily influenced the creation of the provisions were animated by several separate and sometimes opposing goals. Thus Thomas Jefferson, expressing aspects of Enlightenment thinking, believed that the integrity of government could be preserved only by erecting "a wall of separation" between church and state. A sharp division of authority was essential, in his opinion, to insulate the democratic process from ecclesiastical depredations and excursions. James Madison shared this view but also perceived church-state separation as benefiting religious institutions and encouraging a series of competing sects that would ultimately create a benign equilibrium. Even more strongly, Roger Williams—one of the earliest colonial proponents of religious freedom, whose ideas continued forcefully—posited an evangelical theory of separation, believing it was vital to protect the sanctity of the church's "garden" from the "wilderness"

7. See Ronald Dworkin, The Forum of Principle, 56 N.Y.U. L. Rev. 469 (1981).

8. Gey, 52 U. Pitt. L. Rev. at 124. See generally James H. Hutson, The Creation of the Constitution: The Integrity of the Documentary Record, 65 Tex. L. Rev. 1 (1986).

9. Mark Tushnet, Red, White, and Blue 36–37 (1988); Frank H. Easterbrook, Abstraction and Authority, 59 U. Chi. L. Rev. 349, 361–62 (1992).

of the state.[10] It would simply be impossible to satisfy all these purposes in a coherent way with respect to many problems that arise. This difficulty may be highlighted by the fact that there is evidence that one purpose of the Establishment Clause was to protect the existing state-established churches from interference by the newly ordained national government.[11] (Indeed, although disestablishment was then well under way, the epoch of state-sponsored churches did not close until 1833, when Massachusetts finally separated church and state.) Obviously, after application of the Establishment Clause to the states through the Fourteenth Amendment, the fulfillment of this original purpose would be painfully complicated.[12]

Fourth, just as the historical evidence indicates that those responsible for drafting and ratifying the Fourteenth Amendment did not anticipate that its equal protection guarantee would then outlaw racial segregation in public schools,[13] so should rigid insistence on implementing the precise intent of the framers of the First Amendment be avoided. Even if such original thinking is discernible from the often opaque sources, implementing it might jeopardize values that we now perceive as unconditionally secured by the Religion Clauses,[14] assurances that the creators of the Bill of Rights might well have contemplated would eventually be included

10. See Michael E. Smith, The Special Place of Religion in the Constitution, 1983 Sup. Ct. Rev. 83 (noting that at one time or another all of these positions have been reflected in Supreme Court opinions on the Religion Clauses).

11. See Laurence H. Tribe, American Constitutional Law 1161 (2d ed. 1988).

12. See Akhil Reed Amar, The Bill of Rights as a Constitution, 100 Yale L.J. 1131, 1157–58 (1991).

13. Alexander M. Bickel, The Original Understanding and the Segregation Decision, 69 Harv. L. Rev. 1, 58–59 (1955); Michael J. Perry, Interpretivism, Freedom of Expression, and Equal Protection, 42 Ohio St. L.J. 261, 299–300 (1981).

14. See generally Ronald Dworkin, Law's Empire 87–90 (1986); Harry H. Wellington, Interpreting the Constitution: The Supreme Court and the Process of Adjudication chap. 3 (1990).

within their protection.[15] At least in part because our nation has become far more religiously heterogeneous, "practices which may have been objectionable to no one in the time of Jefferson and Madison may today be highly offensive to. . .the deeply devout and the nonbelievers alike."[16]

Fifth, even if the framers' intent were unanimous, unambiguous, and totally in accord with contemporary values, it could provide no ready answers for the resolution of many of today's church-state problems. For example, since public education was virtually nonexistent until long after the Revolution,[17] the founders could have no specific position on the matter of religious activities in the public schools, one of the most frequently litigated and emotionally charged modern Establishment Clause subjects. Nor did the framers foresee the development of such social and regulatory programs as unemployment insurance,[18] antidiscrimination laws,[19] the National Labor Relations Act,[20] or the Fair Labor Standards Act,[21] all of which have generated thorny church-state issues.

The history of the Religion Clauses,[22] like that of most provisions of the Constitution, does not supply a detailed blueprint for resolving issues, drawn from historical intentions that are determinate and identifiable.[23] Nonetheless, it

15. Tushnet, Red, White, and Blue at 34–35; Bickel, 69 Harv. L. Rev. at 63.

16. Schempp, 374 U.S. at 241 (Brennan, J., concurring).

17. See id. at 238 & n. 7.

18. See Sherbert v. Verner, 374 U.S. 398 (1963).

19. See Bob Jones University v. United States, 461 U.S. 574 (1983); Trans-World Airlines, Inc. v. Hardison, 432 U.S. 63 (1977).

20. See NLRB v. Catholic Bishop of Chicago, 440 U.S. 490 (1979).

21. Tony and Susan Alamo Foundation v. Secretary of Labor, 471 U.S. 290 (1985).

22. The historical references in the substantive discussion that follows throughout the book—see, e.g., text at notes 46, 66–70, 92–96 below and chapter 4, note 87—have been selectively chosen not to suggest that the analysis is originally ordained, but rather to indicate some congruity between my thesis and the thoughts of the framers.

23. Tushnet, Red, White, and Blue at 39.

does "divulge a broad philosophy of church-state relations,"[24] articulating a "major premise [that] is a principle or stated value that the ratifiers wanted to protect against hostile legislation or executive action."[25] This historical perspective should be used to fashion reasoned constitutional standards that will address the evils the framers feared, account for the language set down in the document, and reflect cherished contemporary values by a "continuity of identification with those who had proposed and ratified the First Amendment."[26]

JUDICIAL ROLE

This book will deal with the content the Supreme Court should give to the Religion Clauses. I do not intend to explore in any real depth the federal judiciary's capacity to engage in substantive constitutional interpretation or the propriety of its doing so. Nonetheless, as I noted above, certain general considerations about the Court's fitting role in our system of government and its ability to perform it inevitably influence the nature of the constitutional rules it should adopt.

Admittedly, in translating the "broad philosophy" and "major premise" of the Religion Clauses into sensible and workable canons that reflect desirable policy in our religiously diverse nation, the justices must exercise substantial authority of a political (or legislative) nature—"normative" rather than "objective" judgment, "reflective" rather than "determinant" decision making[27]—that will inevitably be shaped by their personal backgrounds, values, and perspectives rather than by some logical analysis. Even assuming that this discretion will not be unbounded by some attachment to the constitutional text and history, and that "judgment always operates

24. Chester J. Antieau, Arthur T. Downey & Edward C. Roberts, Freedom from Federal Establishment xi (1964).

25. Robert H. Bork, The Tempting of America 162–63 (1990). See also Ronald Dworkin, Taking Rights Seriously 134–36 (1977).

26. Robert Post, Theories of Constitutional Interpretation, in Law and the Order of Culture 13, 29 (Robert Post ed. 1991).

27. Immanuel Kant, The Critique of Judgment 466–67 (Encyclopaedia Britannica 1952).

within an institutionally defined structure of opportunities and possibilities,"[28] there will often be such basic disagreements among judges as to produce widely different rules.

Still, whether because the process of constitutional exegesis is legitimated by the fact that its "authority lies in its character as law"[29] or by its ultimately being equated with the "consent of the governed,"[30] in my view one of the major goals in generating intellectually coherent legal principles should be to produce standards[31] that, in application, will work as forcefully as attainable to constrain judges from inserting their own ideological beliefs into constitutional decision making in ad hoc, unreasoned ways.[32] This ideal—endorsed by constitutional theorists and scholars ranging from John Rawls to Antonin Scalia[33]—is especially important under my conception of the appropriate role of an independent judiciary in regard to the ambiguity and judgment inherent in constitutional interpretation.

Consequently, I urge the Court to apply the constitutional rules faithfully and consistently even when doing so

28. Ronald Beiner, Political Judgment 148 (1983).
29. Post, Theories of Constitutional Interpretation at 19.
30. Id. at 21.
31. I use the terms "standards," "rules," and "principles" interchangeably in this context. Compare Kathleen M. Sullivan, The Justices of Rules and Standards, 106 Harv. L. Rev. 22, 56–123 (1992) (distinguishing between "rules" and "standards").
32. It is not unfair to characterize my approach in regard to this matter as acknowledging the inevitability of the justices' "legislating wholesale" when fashioning broad principles but still seeking to avoid their "legislating retail" in day-to-day administration of these rules.
33. John Rawls, A Theory of Justice 235–43 (1971); Antonin Scalia, The Rule of Law as a Law of Rules, 56 U. Chi. L. Rev. 1175 (1989). See also, e.g., Frank H. Easterbrook, The Court and the Economic System, 98 Harv. L. Rev. 4 (1984); Charles Fried, Two Concepts of Interests: Some Reflections on the Supreme Court's Balancing Test, 76 Harv. L. Rev. 755 (1963); Frederick Schauer, Playing by the Rules: A Philosophical Examination of Rule-Based Decision-Making in Law and in Life 149–55, 231–32 (1991). Compare Duncan Kennedy, Form and Substance in Private Law Adjudication, 89 Harv. L. Rev. 1685, 1737–66 (1976); Morton J. Horwitz, The Rule of Law: An Unqualified Human Good? 86 Yale L.J. 561 (1977); Frank I. Michelman, Traces of Self-Government, 100 Harv. L. Rev. 4 (1988).

may require the justices either to invalidate specific practices
that were apparently approved by those who gave us the
fundamental law[34] or to decline to reject laws that seem
plainly to be at war with primary constitutional values that
should have stopped conscientious government officials from
enacting them in the first place.[35] An optimum thesis should
produce as few such results as possible—ideally none at all.
But acknowledging that many readers will disagree, I am willing to have my proposed principles be short of flawless on
this score in order to achieve other urgent needs.

I agree with Frank Easterbrook's persuasively developed
yet simply stated conclusion that in developing rules for constitutional decision making the Court "should search for that
degree of generality capable of justifying a *judicial* role."[36] In
this respect, in crafting admittedly imperfect standards *for
judicial enforcement,* I believe that the central concern should
be for realistic abridgments of constitutionally secured liberty
rather than for hyperbolic potentialities. Indeed, in my view
there is a lesser evil in those rules that fail to nullify extreme
actions that appear to abridge basic precepts than in those
that disapprove programs long embedded in our traditions.
Hypothetical government regulations that fall in the former
category are of less concern because experience reveals that
there is a wide gap between conjuring up aggravated possibilities and enacting laws that are plainly unconstitutional. Although not inconceivable, for a patent violation of the nation's fundamental charter to occur requires that it overcome
all the hurdles of lawmaking (and review) by persons who,
like justices of the United States Supreme Court, have sworn
to uphold the Constitution. As for the latter category, that

34. See Michael W. McConnell, On Reading the Constitution, 73
Corn. L. Rev. 359, 362–63 (1988). It may be reasonably argued, however,
that the founders did not intend that their original judgment should be
unaffected by political developments and judicial decisions over the years.
See Robert W. Bennett, Objectivity in Constitutional Law, 132 U. Pa. L.
Rev. 445, 456–74 (1984).

35. See pp. 157–58 below for discussion of such an extreme, but unlikely, hypothetical.

36. Easterbrook, 59 U. Chi. L. Rev. at 372.

certain government practices have gained wide acceptance because they have been in place for many years does not ensure their conformity to the preservation of personal freedoms guaranteed by the Constitution.

Finally, as a more specific example of my intent to make some observations about the broader role of the Supreme Court in the course of discussing a desirable interpretation of the Religion Clauses: although some content must be given to the term "religion" for purposes of the First Amendment, since most judges are neither theologians nor philosophers, I think it would be most undesirable to construct a judicial definition whose administration would require a deep understanding of these disciplines.

UNDERLYING VALUES

As I will explain more fully below, I believe that the dominant theme (the "major premise") of both Religion Clauses is to protect religious liberty and the integrity of individual conscience, and that *judicial enforcement of these provisions should be confined to securing those freedoms.* Since the essential function of judicial review, in my opinion, is to protect personal liberty, especially for minorities who do not receive vigorous representation in the political process,[37] and since the most frequent threats to religious freedom will be made against groups outside the mainstream, I propose an energetic role for the Court in this area.

The traditional "liberal" view, expounded most faithfully in recent decades by Justice Brennan (and adhered to by Justice Marshall), has been the most activist. It has provided a generous interpretation of the Free Exercise Clause, usually affording members of religious minorities an exemption from generally applicable government regulations that conflict with the tenets of their faith.[38] At the same time, it has ordinarily given the Establishment Clause a "separationist"

37. See Jesse H. Choper, Judicial Review and the National Political Process 64 (1980).

38. See, e.g., Hobbie v. Unemployment Appeals Commission, 480 U.S. 136 (1987).

emphasis,[39] limiting the power of the mainstream Judeo-Christian sects[40] to use government to achieve their ends, except in some instances when a more "accommodationist" version was needed to uphold legislative solicitude for religious freedom (which tended to benefit minority faiths as well as the more influential ones).[41] On the other hand, the conventional "conservative" position, most recently led by Justice Scalia (regularly joined by Chief Justice Rehnquist and Justice White), has been almost totally deferential, rejecting free exercise claims by religious minorities[42] and refusing Establishment Clause challenges to government programs that benefit mainstream religions.[43]

I believe that the several postulates advanced by Justice Brennan cannot be reconciled and, in addition, are not adequately sympathetic to the sensibilities of the nation's mainstream religions. I also feel that Justice Scalia's stance is unduly insensitive to the needs of our country's smaller sects. My proposed thesis rests somewhere between these positions, but it is by no means put forward as a doctrinal or political

39. See, e.g., Grand Rapids School District v. Ball, 473 U.S. 373 (1985).

40. Among the more than one thousand different religions in the United States, see J. Gordon Melton, The Encyclopedia of American Religions (3d ed. 1989) (describing 1,588 religious groups in this country and Canada), I include in the term "mainstream" those defined by a recent study as "Protestantism as it finds expression among the Baptists, the Methodists, the Episcopalians, the Presbyterians, the Congregationalists, the Disciples of Christ, and the Lutherans, as well as the other two 'great faiths,' Catholicism and Judaism," in contrast to "groups that have been called 'marginal' or 'non-normative' or 'cults' in their history, such as Mormons and Christian Scientists, Spiritualists and Theosophists, followers of Meher Baba or the Reverend Sun Myung Moon, practitioners of Hare Krishna, feminist witchcraft, or Zen." Mary F. Bednarowski, American Religion: A Cultural Perspective 3 (1984). A more succinct description is "the dominant, culturally established faiths held by the majority of Americans." Wade C. Roof & William McKinney, American Mainline Religion: Its Changing Shape and Future 6 (1987).

41. See, e.g., Corporation of the Presiding Bishop v. Amos, 483 U.S. 327, 340 (1987) (Brennan, J., concurring).

42. See, e.g., Employment Division v. Smith, 494 U.S. 872 (1990).

43. See, e.g., Lee v. Weisman, 112 S.Ct. 2649, 2678 (1992) (Scalia, J., dissenting); Allegheny County v. ACLU, 492 U.S. 573 (1989); Bowen v. Kendrick, 487 U.S. 589 (1988).

compromise. Rather, although it will surely be unacceptable to all existing major interest groups and will likely be found objectionable on some score by most interested observers, I believe it more effectively secures religious liberty for all.

Many of the judgments expressed above obviously reflect personal values that inevitably influence constitutional rule making. In this book I shall self-consciously identify those points along the way where predilection rather than logic provides a significant link in the discussion and where difficult questions are being resolved in the face of strong countervailing arguments. By directly informing readers when these factors are at work, I want to afford them the opportunity to modify my analysis accordingly, in the hope that they may find it sufficiently useful so as not to reject the thesis in its entirety even though they may be unsatisfied by some or all of the proposed principles and their supporting discussion.[44]

THE CORE VALUE OF RELIGIOUS LIBERTY

Although it may be that a perceptive observer's conclusion that "liberty is the end, the goal, and the entire rationale of what the First Amendment says about religion"[45] is an overstatement, there is general—it is fair to say nearly universal—agreement that the paramount concern of both Religion Clauses is to protect religious liberty: the freedom to pursue (or not to choose) a religious faith. This central tenet was the

44. Probably the two most idiosyncratic—and consequently controversial—propositions concern (a) the limited definition of religious beliefs that will benefit from the special protection of the Free Exercise Clause urged in chapter 3, and (b) the largely inflexible prohibition under the Establishment Clause against most forms of government financial assistance for religion—outlined at pp. 16–19 of this chapter and illustrated more fully in chapter 5—even when this monetary aid is seemingly offered in the service of religious liberty. I believe that either of these rules (and many others) may be significantly altered while still preserving the essence of my thesis. For example, see pp. 80–83, 85 below.

45. Richard John Neuhaus, A New Order of Religious Freedom, 60 Geo. Wash. L. Rev. 620, 626–27 (1992).

object of the provisions' prime architect,[46] represented the "core value of the religion clauses. . .throughout American history from the colonial period of Roger Williams to the early national period of the Founders,"[47] has been supported by textual construction of the First Amendment,[48] and enjoys the concurrence of virtually every major church-state commentator—whether separationist, accommodationist, or centrist[49]—and every justice of the Supreme Court who has expressed some opinion on the subject.[50] Although this freedom may serve various ancillary objectives, including the individual rights of autonomy and self-expression or the community right of religious groups to foster the virtues of civic republicanism,[51] its preeminence is granted.

OVERLAP OF THE CLAUSES

If religious liberty could be secured by a reasonable interpretation of the Free Exercise Clause alone, it would be fair to contend that my analysis—which makes this freedom the fundamental goal of both Religion Clauses (and which conditions judicial enforcement on its being significantly endan-

46. See, e.g., Paul J. Weber, James Madison and Religious Equality: The Perfect Separation, 44 Rev. Pol. 163, 175 (1982).

47. Arlin M. Adams & Charles J. Emmerich, A Heritage of Religious Liberty, 137 U. Pa. L. Rev. 1559, 1643 (1989).

48. Mary Ann Glendon & Raul F. Yanes, Structural Free Exercise, 90 Mich. L. Rev. 477, 541 (1991).

49. See, e.g., Leo Pfeffer, Church, State, and Freedom 122 (1953); Paul G. Kauper, Religion and the Constitution 77 (1964); Wilber G. Katz, Freedom of Religion and State Neutrality, 20 U. Chi. L. Rev. 426, 428 (1953); Philip B. Kurland, Of Church and State and the Supreme Court, 29 U. Chi. L. Rev. 1, 4 (1961); Tribe, American Constitutional Law at 1160–61, 1201–4; Michael W. McConnell, Accommodation of Religion, 60 Geo. Wash. L. Rev. 685, 690 (1992); Douglas Laycock, The Benefits of the Establishment Clauses, 42 De Paul L. Rev. 373 (1990); Steven L. Carter, The Resurrection of Religious Freedom? 107 Harv. L. Rev. 118, 134 (1993).

50. See, e.g., Wallace v. Jaffree, 472 U.S. 38, 48–55 (1985) (Stevens, J.); Schempp, 374 U.S. at 305 (Goldberg, J., concurring); id. at 227 (Douglas, J., concurring); id. at 232 (Brennan, J., concurring); Everson, 330 U.S. at 8–11 (opinion of the Court by Black, J.); id. at 53–54 (Rutledge, J., dissenting).

51. See Timothy L. Hall, Religion and Civic Virtue: A Justification of Free Exercise, 67 Tul. L. Rev. 87 (1992).

gered)—renders the Establishment Clause "redundant,"[52] "mere surplusage,"[53] or "a virtual nullity."[54] It would be no more persuasive, however, than many other analogous points that might be made: for example, that a fair construction of the Due Process Clause might eliminate the utility of the Equal Protection Clause,[55] or that a plausible reading of the Takings Clause might cover all that the Contracts Clause was meant to accomplish. Nonetheless, although it is by no means analytically indispensable to give each of the Religion Clauses a distinct task and emphasis in building a comprehensive thesis, it will be both helpful and consistent with the framers' view that "the nonestablishment and free exercise guarantees play different, although mutually supportive, roles in protecting religious liberty."[56]

The set of principles I will elaborate in subsequent chapters interprets each of the Religion Clauses as follows. The Free Exercise Clause protects adherents of religious faiths and nonbelievers from government action that either hostilely singles them out for the imposition of adverse consequences or, although benignly motivated, has the effect of burdening religious observers because of action or inaction mandated by the precepts of their faith. In the main, it prevents the state from *impeding* the practices of religious minorities that are either disfavored or unacknowledged by the majority. When the Court holds that intentional discrimination against persons with certain religious beliefs is unconstitutional, the offensive provision of the law is wholly invalid. But when it finds a violation of the Free Exercise Clause on the second ground (burdensome effect), this will usually mean that the law is invalid only as applied; all that is required is an exemption for the claimant from the regulation's

52. Suzanna A. Sherry, Lee v. Weisman, Paradox Redux, 1992 Sup. Ct. Rev. 123, 138.

53. See Kathleen M. Sullivan, Religion and Liberal Democracy, 59 U. Chi. L. Rev. 195, 205 (1992).

54. Lee v. Weisman, 112 S.Ct. at 2673 (Souter, J., concurring).

55. See Bolling v. Sharpe 347 U.S. 497 (1954); Peter Westen, The Empty Idea of Equality, 95 Harv. L. Rev. 537, 558–59 n. 69 (1982).

56. Adams & Emmerich, 137 U. Pa. L. Rev. at 1604.

otherwise proper operation. In contrast, the major thrust of the Establishment Clause concerns government action whose intent or independent impact[57] *favors* religion even though its overall effect often may be much broader. Such types of laws may meaningfully threaten religious liberty (and thus be impermissible under my thesis) in several ways. Usually they do so by promoting "the majority's favored brand of religion."[58] But government action that seeks to assist minority faiths may also undermine religious freedom by posing the danger that *believers and nonbelievers* alike will be required to support their own religious observance or that of others. When the Court finds a violation of the Establishment Clause, this will often mean that the offensive law is invalid in its entirety and may not be enforced at all. Sometimes, however, only that part of a general government program that improperly advances religion must be eliminated. In these ways the two religion provisions of the First Amendment will "work together in the service of religious liberty."[59]

SIGNIFICANT DANGERS

It is much easier to identify the Religion Clauses' core value of protecting religious liberty than to describe precisely

57. The terms "intent" and "independent impact" will be defined more fully below. They replace other phrases used in my previous writings on this subject, where I referred either to "religious purpose," 56 Calif. L. Rev. 260, 268 (1968); 27 Wm. & Mary L. Rev. 943, 948 (1986); 29 Ariz. L. Rev. 551, 552 (1987) or to "solely religious" purpose, 47 Minn. L. Rev. 329, 330 (1963); 41 U. Pitt. L. Rev. 673, 675 (1980). In discussing the matter, I sought to emphasize that "the crux of this delicate inquiry into why a majority of legislators enacted a particular law is best evidenced by its primary (or independent) effect." 1982 U. Ill. L. Rev. 579, 607; see also 56 Calif. L. Rev. at 277–83.

The matter of ascertaining legislative intention is explored in some detail in chapters 2 and 4. The terms "intent," "purpose," and "motive" will generally be used interchangeably throughout the relevant discussion. In so doing, I do not mean in any way to enter the recently renewed debate on methods of interpreting the output of the lawmaking process. See generally Daniel B. Rodriguez, The Substance of the New Legal Process, 77 Calif. L. Rev. 919, 928–33 (1989).

58. McConnell, 60 Geo. Wash. L. Rev. at 690.

59. Glendon & Yanes, 90 Mich. L. Rev. at 482.

the kinds of government-produced threats to that freedom that are forbidden by the First Amendment. Further discussion throughout the book will reveal that resolution of the problem depends on the context and hinges in part on value-influenced conclusions of law[60] and in part on empirical inquiries on which people may reasonably disagree.[61] Two major forms, however, will be considered here.

Discrimination

When government deliberately (either explicitly or covertly) selects persons or groups for adverse treatment (whether criminal punishment or denial of civil benefits) because they do or do not hold certain religious beliefs or do or do not engage in certain practices because of their faith, this places an identifiable cost or burden on their right of free religious choice. In contrast to singling out (discriminating against) persons because of some activity unconnected with their system of belief (e.g., their occupation), equal treatment of religion, as will be developed in detail, is a crucial concern of the First Amendment, recently depicted by the Court as a "bedrock" principle: "regardless of history, government may not demonstrate a preference for a particular faith."[62] In my view, if government intentionally exacts a charge on people for the exercise of their individual religion, this constitutes a meaningful threat to religious liberty even if the punishment, cost, or burden is not substantial enough to coerce or influence them to compromise or abandon their precepts.[63] Discrimination by government based on one's possessing (or not having) a certain faith imposes a penalty on religious prerogative and interferes with true religious freedom whether or not "the religious decisions of the people will be distorted"

60. These are stated most specifically at pp. 117–19 below.
61. See especially chapter 4, notes 134 and 159 below.
62. Allegheny County v. ACLU, 492 U.S. 593, 605 (1989).
63. Compare Ira C. Lupu, Reconstructing the Establishment Clause: The Case against Discretionary Accommodation of Religion, 140 U. Pa. L. Rev. 555, 567, 579 (1991).

or real "disincentives to religious practice are created"[64] by the government action.[65]

In addition to purposeful inequality, the right of voluntary religious choice may also be seriously undermined by generally applicable government regulations that conflict with the dictates of some faiths, thus discriminating against certain religions in effect, though not by design. This too will be the subject of extended consideration in this book.

Tax Support

There is broad consensus that a central threat to the religious freedom of individuals and groups—indeed, in the judgment of many, "the most serious infringement upon religious liberty"[66]—is posed "by forcing them to pay taxes in support of a religious establishment or religious activities."[67] This is cogently confirmed by Thomas Jefferson's "Virginia Bill for Religious Liberty," which proclaimed that "to compel a man to furnish contributions of money for the propagation of opinions which he disbelieves, is sinful and tyrannical";[68] by James Madison's "Memorial and Remonstrance against Religious Assessments" (whose title is itself revealing), which condemned even forcing "a citizen to contribute three pence only of his property" to support any religious establish-

64. McConnell, 60 Geo. Wash. L. Rev. at 733 n. 212.

65. In addition, the public welfare in general may suffer harm as a result of certain kinds of actions that believers may feel required to take in order to avoid violating their religious principles. See Timothy L. Hall, Sacred Solemnity: Civic Prayer, Civil Communion, and the Establishment Clause, 79 Iowa L. Rev. 35 (1993).

66. Leo Pfeffer, Some Current Issues in Church and State, 13 W. Res. L. Rev. 9, 18 (1961); see also Flast v. Gardner, 271 F. Supp. 1 (S.D.N.Y. 1967) (Frankel, J., dissenting): "It is now familiar to all who have touched this subject that a central concern—perhaps the most central concern—of the Establishment Clause is to ban utterly the use of public moneys to support any religion or all religions." See generally Leonard W. Levy, The Establishment Clause: Religion and the First Amendment (1986); Adams & Emmerich, 137 U. Pa. L. Rev. at 1620–21.

67. Paul G. Kauper, Church and State: Cooperative Separatism, 60 Mich. L. Rev. 1, 9 (1961). See also id. at 5–6.

68. 12 Hening, Statutes of Virginia 84 (1823). But cf. Mark deW. Howe, The Garden and the Wilderness 26 (1965).

ment;[69] by Thomas Cooley's *Constitutional Limitations,* which found clearly unlawful "under any of the American constitutions. . .compulsory support, by taxation or otherwise, of religious instruction";[70] and by many important Supreme Court opinions in the church-state field—majority, concurring, dissenting[71]—beginning with the Court's first major interpretation of the Establishment Clause[72] in which the justices, unanimously emphasizing the "conviction that individual religious liberty could be achieved best under a government which was stripped of all power to tax, to support, or otherwise to assist any or all religions,"[73] reasoned that the nonestablishment provision meant at least that "no tax in any amount, large or small, can be levied to support any religious activities or institutions, whatever they may be called, or whatever form they may adopt to teach or practice religion."[74] Although public subsidy of religion may not directly influence people's beliefs or practices, it plainly coerces taxpayers either to contribute indirectly to their religions or, even worse, to support sectarian doctrines and causes that are antithetical to their own convictions. As a matter of both historical design[75]

69. ¶ 3, set forth in Everson, 330 U.S. at 65–66 (1947) (app.). See also Leo Pfeffer, Federal Funds for Parochial Schools? No, 37 Notre Dame Law. 309, 310–11 (1962); Flast, 271 F. Supp. at 6–7 (Frankel, J., dissenting): " 'Support' by use of taxpayers' money lay at the heart of Jefferson's and Madison's concern."

70. Thomas M. Cooley, A Treatise on the Constitutional Limitations 663–64 (7th ed. 1903).

71. See, e.g., Engel v. Vitale, 370 U.S. 421, 442 n. 7 (1962) (Douglas, J., concurring); McGowan v. Maryland, 336 U.S. 420, 453 (1961) (opinion of the Court by Warren, C.J.); McCollum v. Board of Education, 333 U.S. 203, 248, 249 (1948) (Reed, J., dissenting); Everson, 330 U.S. at 8, 10–12 (opinion of the Court by Black, J.); id. at 33, 41, 44, 52, 53 (Rutledge, J., dissenting).

72. For an earlier discussion, see Terrett v. Taylor, 13 U.S. (9 Cranch) 43, 48–49 (1815).

73. Everson, 330 U.S. at 11.

74. Id. at 15.

75. "The coercion that was a hallmark of historical establishments of religion was coercion of religious orthodoxy and of financial support by force of law and threat of penalty." Lee v. Weisman, 112 S.Ct. at 2683 (1992) (Scalia, J., dissenting) (emphasis omitted). See also Thomas J. Curry, The First Freedoms: Church and State in America to the Passage of the

and present constitutional policy, the Religion Clauses—
particularly the Establishment Clause—should, in my view,
forbid so basic an infringement of religious liberty.[76]

Just as there is a large difference between persecuting
people because of their religious beliefs and merely requiring
them to contribute funds to churches, so too there are varying
degrees of gravity in respect to compelled financial support.
Thus it is often argued that, especially in view of the historical
aversion to "religious assessments," a distinction should be
drawn under the Religion Clauses between direct government subsidies and tax exemptions.[77] Similarly, one might
reasonably distinguish between financial support through
spending programs (whether in the form of direct grants or
tax exemptions) and the seemingly more focused aid provided through the welfare system (for example, unemployment compensation or social security payments).

In fact, as subsequent discussion will show, it may well be
that drawing the line at one of these points (or some other)

First Amendment 147, 217 (1986) (taxation to support religion believed to
violate religious freedom).

76. The existence of an *individual* right not to have one's compulsorily
raised tax funds spent for religious purposes explains the Court's decision
in Flast v. Cohen, 392 U.S. 83 (1968), granting federal taxpayers standing
to challenge federal expenditures allegedly in violation of the Religion
Clauses. As the Court put it: "Our history vividly illustrates that one of the
specific evils feared by those who drafted the Establishment Clause and
fought for its adoption was that the taxing and spending power would be
used to favor one religion over another or to support religion in general.
. . .The concern of Madison and his supporters was quite clearly that religious liberty ultimately would be the victim." 392 U.S. at 103. See also
Stewart, J., concurring: "Because [the Establishment Clause] plainly prohibits taxing and spending in aid of religion, every taxpayer can claim a personal constitutional right not to be taxed for the support of a religious
institution." 392 U.S. at 114. Finally, Justice Harlan's dissent, 392 U.S. at
125, acknowledged the essence of the Court's reasoning "that a taxpayer's
claim under the Establishment Clause is 'not merely one of ultra vires,' but
one which instead asserts 'an abridgment of individual religious liberty'
and a 'governmental infringement of individual rights protected by the
Constitution,'" citing Jesse H. Choper, The Establishment Clause and Aid
to Parochial Schools, 56 Calif. L. Rev. 260, 276 (1968).

77. See Boris I. Bittker, Churches, Taxes and the Constitution, 78 Yale
L.J. 1285 (1969); William R. Consedine & Charles M. Whelan, Church Tax
Exemptions, 15 Cath. Law. 93 (1969).

produces results that would be more comfortable for many people (including me) than those of the alternatives.[78] But putting policy considerations of this kind aside, I believe it is analytically unsatisfactory to treat these financial benefits differently, particularly because of the augmented burdens of taxation and the increased creation of "new property" through the expanded welfare state. The similarities among these various forms of monetary assistance seem to me to call for equivalent treatment. This argument is especially persuasive because tax exemptions for religious activities usually force other taxpayers to account for the lost revenue in precisely the same amount,[79] and the case is particularly vivid when money is actually being transferred from the government to the individual, which confers a financial benefit on the recipient of exactly the value of the economic cost to the state.[80]

DIFFERENT APPROACHES

Although there is little disagreement with the core proposition that preservation of religious liberty is the dominant concern of the Constitution's provisions on religion, a variety of persuasive theories have been propounded that take different account of this central value. These should be reviewed because of their potential effect on any comprehensive set of rules for governing disputes that arise under the Religion Clauses. Although their deficiencies (as well as their strengths) will be highlighted here, the improvements that my thesis seeks to achieve will be developed in the chapters that follow.

NEUTRALITY

The concept of neutrality has been influential in regard to approaches governing the constitutional separation of church

78. These results are dictated by the second controversial proposition described in note 44 above.

79. Michael W. McConnell & Richard A. Posner, An Economic Approach to Issues of Religious Freedom, 56 U. Chi. L. Rev. 1, 12 (1989).

80. This is explained more fully at pp. 123–26 below.

and state. The idea of no official preference for one religion over another, or for religion over irreligion,[81] responds to our nation's strong general commitment to equality. But the principle of neutrality may be formulated in a variety of ways,[82] and the abstract notion of equality demands further content. The version of the doctrine urged most prominently by Philip Kurland—"that government cannot utilize religion as a standard for action or inaction"[83]—adds an important ingredient to the precept that religion may not be *favored* over irreligion: religion also may not be *disfavored* in comparison with *other similarly situated* groups. Beyond its intuitively appealing symmetry and its adherence to the valued idea of evenhandedness,[84] this rule of "religion blindness" alleviates substantial problems that are present under other approaches, including mine. Most notably, it often eliminates the need to define "religion";[85] such definition may be avoided as long as the government benefits or burdens are

81. The contention of Chief Justice Rehnquist that "the Establishment Clause did not require government neutrality between religion and irreligion nor did it prohibit the Federal Government from providing nondiscriminatory aid to religion"—Jaffree, 472 U.S. at 106 (Rehnquist, J., dissenting), based largely on the historical work of Robert L. Cord, Separation of Church and State: Historical Fact and Current Fiction (1982), and Michael J. Malbin, Religion and Politics: The Intentions of the Authors of the First Amendment 1–17 (1978)—has been forcefully challenged by Levy, The Establishment Clause at 91–119, and Douglas Laycock, "Nonpreferential" Aid to Religion: A False Claim about Original Intent, 27 Wm. & Mary L. Rev. 875, 882–83 (1986) and does not appear to have been a matter of serious consideration since the mid-1980s.

82. See Tribe, American Constitutional Law at 1188–1201.

83. Kurland, 29 U. Chi. L. Rev. at 6.

84. This definition of "neutrality" has recently been dubbed "formal" neutrality, in contrast to "what might be called substantive neutrality, which. . .would generally require government to accommodate religious differences by exempting religious practices from formally neutral laws. See generally Douglas Laycock, Formal, Substantive, and Disaggregated Neutrality toward Religion, 39 De Paul L. Rev. 993 (1990)." Church of the Lukumi Babalu Aye, Inc. v. Hialeah, 113 S.Ct. 2217, 2241–42 (Souter, J., concurring).

85. This complex and extraordinarily delicate task will be discussed in chapter 3.

distributed more broadly, that is, so long as "religion" is included within a sufficiently larger category.[86]

Despite its inherent attraction and significant advantages, I believe the neutrality approach has two serious shortcomings: the rule both produces results hostile to religious liberty without serving nonestablishment values and also permits forms of aid that subvert historical and contemporary aims of the Establishment Clause.

The neutrality approach is inadequately sensitive to religious freedom by flatly prohibiting all religious exemptions from general regulations no matter how greatly they burden religious exercise and how insubstantial the competing state interest may be. In advancing the admirable goals of government neutrality and impartiality, it downgrades the positive value that both Religion Clauses assign to religious liberty. Consider the following illustration. Suppose that a public school regulation requires pupils to wear shorts during gym class for the aesthetic effect of uniform dress, and that one child requests an exemption because her religious scruples forbid her to bare her legs.[87] The "religion blindness" rule would allow a broadly worded exemption for "all children whose modesty makes the wearing of shorts uncomfortable" or for "all children whose parents request exemption." Either of these would protect the religious objector, but enough other children might also take advantage of the exemption so as to destroy the regulation's aesthetic goal. (The chances that a more inclusive excusal provision would subvert the state's general regulatory interest are even greater, of course, when the burden imposed by the government rule is harsher than just having to wear gym shorts.) Even if the school believed it could excuse the small number of children who objected on religious grounds and still achieve its overall effect of uniform dress, such exemption would constitute an imper-

86. See John H. Mansfield, Book Review, 52 Calif. L. Rev. 212, 215–16 (1964), for the point that the neutrality approach does not wholly relieve the difficulty of defining religion.

87. See Mitchell v. McCall, 273 Ala. 604, 143 So.2d 629 (1962).

missible classification under the neutrality approach. Thus the school board would seemingly be faced with the choice of either protecting the religious child by abandoning its concededly valid program or penalizing her beliefs even though denying the exemption is unnecessary to serve its purpose.[88]

Paradoxically, the neutrality approach not only requires burdens on religious freedom that are at odds with the values of the Free Exercise Clause, but also permits (and indeed may demand) aid to religion that I believe plainly conflicts with objectives of the Establishment Clause. Three examples dramatically reveal how the neutrality approach would allow (and usually require) the use of tax funds for the purely religious functions of church organizations, as long as the legislative classification was broad enough. First, suppose the state allocated public money to private associations for the purpose of distributing replicas of their insignia to their members. The Rotary Club, the League of Women Voters, and religious groups would all be beneficiaries. Under the "religion blindness" rule, denying funds to sectarian organizations would constitute an impermissible religious classification, yet including such groups would designate tax funds to be used to purchase Latin crosses and Stars of David. Second, suppose the state appropriated money for new structures to house voluntary associations. Under the neutrality approach, churches and synagogues would have to be included. The breadth of the classification—using tax funds to support buildings for the United Way and the Chamber of Commerce

88. It may be that a narrower exemption—e.g., for "all children whose parents have strong philosophic or conscientious objections to wearing shorts"—would both satisfy the religion blindness criterion and limit the adverse effect on the school's desire for uniform appearance. But it is equally possible that this sort of classification, although meaningful in some contexts—such as military service, see Welsh v. United States, 398 U.S. 333, 344 (1970) (Harlan, J., concurring) or child rearing, see p. 116 below— either would not, in the gym shorts setting, realistically meet the "breadth" requirement of the neutrality approach because it would be actually confined to religious dissenters or, if applied broadly enough, would permit too many pupils to be excused.

in addition to mainstream (and minority) religions—would seem to many people only to add pocketbook insult to constitutional injury. Finally, suppose the government sought to address the problem of teenage motherhood by underwriting the costs of any organization, public or private, that developed an effective educational program to prevent young girls from becoming pregnant.[89] The Roman Catholic Church could obviously qualify as a recipient under the neutrality approach even though it accomplished the desired end by proselytizing its deeply rooted religious views of abstinence. Indeed, this approach leads logically to the conclusion that, under certain conditions, the government *must* support the spread of religious ideology: Under present constitutional law doctrine, "the government can encourage discussion of politics without favoring one point over another." If the government were to sponsor dissemination of various philosophies and opinions, since "an exclusion of religion is inevitably viewpoint-based," it would "be subject to the most exacting scrutiny"; thus, "provided that religion is not singled out for special support—i.e., that comparable secular institutions are included in the program— . . . government support from general revenues"[90] would plainly follow.

It may be that as a matter of public policy and analytic reasoning these results are as they should be. Neither generally understood history nor widely shared values necessarily compel a contrary conclusion. In my view, however, the neutrality approach would allow—indeed demand—state advancement and support of religion well beyond what *should* be encompassed within our tradition of church-state separation.[91]

89. See Bowen v. Kendrick, 487 U.S. 589 (1988).
90. Michael W. McConnell, Political and Religious Disestablishment, 1986 B.Y.U. L. Rev. 405, 419, 452.
91. If our economy were to reach such a stage of collectivization that government fiscal polices so shrank private sources of funds as to make voluntary support of religion impracticable, there might then be merit in reevaluating the historically rooted and contemporarily valued prohibition against state support of strictly sectarian activities. See Donald A. Giannella, Religious Liberty, Nonestablishment and Doctrinal Development (pt. 2): The Nonestablishment Principle, 81 Harv. L. Rev. 513, 522–26, 537–55

I believe that the Constitution calls for religion to be treated *specially*, and that this means more than that religion must be treated *equally* (although a constitutional requirement of equality itself makes religion special, since a strict rule of nondiscrimination is applicable to only a small number of subjects). As already indicated, I believe that under the Free Exercise Clause religion must sometimes be afforded special privilege ("preferred" is not an inaccurate term), and that under the Establishment Clause religion must sometimes be subject to special limits ("disfavored" is not an unfair term). Unfortunately, these principles will generate a tension between the two Religion Clauses that the neutrality approach commendably avoids. But, as will be seen, resolving the conflict is not an insuperable task. Finally, I agree that our constitutional tradition (and government system) would be well served by moving in the direction of equal treatment of political and religious ideologies. As we shall see, however, I believe that *less* support of *all* ideologies would be the better principle and the wiser course.

DIVISIVENESS

Another influential precept, grounded in the views of thinkers such as John Locke[92] and Roger Williams,[93] urges that a primary function of the Religion Clauses is "to keep bitter religious controversy out of public life by denying to every denomination any advantage from getting control of public policy or the public purse."[94] This postulate has appeared quite prominently in Supreme Court opinions.[95]

(1968); William W. Van Alstyne, Constitutional Separation of Church and State: The Quest for a Coherent Position, 57 Am. Pol. Sci. Rev. 865, 881–82 (1963). But I do not believe that time has come.

92. John Locke, A Letter concerning Toleration, in John Locke: On Politics and Education 34 (Howard R. Penniman ed. 1947).

93. Roger Williams, The Bloudy Tenent of Persecution, in 3 The Complete Writings of Roger Williams 113–17 (Samuel L. Caldwell ed. 1963).

94. Everson, 330 U.S. at 27 (Jackson, J., dissenting). See also McCollum, 333 U.S. at 228 (Frankfurter, J., concurring).

95. In addition to cases cited in note 94, see Larson v. Valente, 456 U.S. 228, 253 (1982) (finding that a state charitable solicitation statute that

In my judgment, however, avoidance of political strife along religious lines neither should nor can represent a value to be judicially secured through the Religion Clauses. Indeed, if government were actually to ban religious conflict in the lawmaking process, this would raise serious questions under the First Amendment's guarantee of political freedom as well as religious liberty.[96]

Practical considerations, however, even more than doctrinal ones, demonstrate the futility of making "political divisiveness" a constitutional determinant under the Religion Clauses. Surely legislation is not invalid simply because a religious organization supported or opposed it. Conflict among sectarian groups in regard to proposed legislation that immediately affects religion—for example, whether public funds should be granted to religious organizations or whether a religious exemption should be afforded from laws of general application—may well be unfortunate. But such discord is neither meaningfully different from nor more dangerous than the disagreements among religious groups that are inevitably generated when government pursues many concededly secular ends. Sectarian organizations have differed concern-

exempted certain religious organizations, but not others, from registration and reporting requirements engendered "a risk of politicizing religion"); Walz v. Tax Commission, 397 U.S. 664, 694 (1970) (Harlan, J., concurring) ("government involvement in religious life . . . is apt to lead to strife and frequently strain a political system to the breaking point"); Board of Education v. Allen, 392 U.S. 236, 254 (1968) (Black, J., dissenting) ("The First Amendment's prohibition against government establishment of religion was written on the assumption that state aid to religion and religious schools generates discord, disharmony, hatred, and strife among our people"); Aguilar v. Felton, 473 U.S. 402, 414 (1985) (noting "the dangers of political divisiveness along religious lines"); Grand Rapids School District v. Ball, 473 U.S. 373, 383 (1985) (referring to the "divisive rifts along religious lines in the body politic" caused by government activity relating to education of children); Lemon v. Kurtzman, 403 U.S. 602, 622 (1971) ("Ordinarily political debate and division, however vigorous or even partisan, are normal and healthy manifestations of our democratic system of government, but political division along religious lines was one of the principal evils against which the First Amendment was intended to protect").

96. See McDaniel v. Paty, 435 U.S. 618 (1978) (unanimously invalidating a state ban on members of the clergy's being state legislators).

ing a wide variety of political issues—including Sunday closing, gambling, pornography, drug control, gun control, conscription, prohibition, abolition of slavery, racial integration,
prostitution, overpopulation, sterilization, abortion, birth
control, marriage, divorce, the Equal Rights Amendment,
and capital punishment, to name but a few. Undoubtedly,
organized churches and other religious groups have markedly influenced the resolution of some of these issues.[97]

As we shall see, the participation of such forces in the
legislative process may well raise the possibility that the intent
or impact of the resulting government action should be subject to special scrutiny because it favors religion. But if a
law serves genuinely secular purposes, or impairs no one's
religious liberty, there is no persuasive reason to hold it unconstitutional simply because its proponents and opponents
were divided along religious lines.

Furthermore, even if government could or should eliminate political dissension because of sectarian differences, the
Religion Clauses would not be a very effective tool for the
task. For example, forbidding laws granting aid to parochial
schools might well ameliorate the "political fragmentation
and divisiveness on religion lines" that could result from "suc-
cessive and very likely permanent annual appropriations that
benefit relatively few religious groups."[98] But this would not
effect a truce; it would only move the battleground. There is
good reason to believe that the failure to assist church-related
schools antagonizes many citizens, who feel that their taxes
are being used to subsidize an alien dogma of secularism.[99]

97. See Center for the Study of Democratic Institutions, Religion and
American Society 71 (1961); Howe, The Garden and the Wilderness at 62;
Kauper, Religion and the Constitution at 83–85; Robert B. Fowler, Religion
and Politics in America (1985); A. James Reichley, Religion in American
Public Life (1985); Jon Butler, Awash in a Sea of Faith: Christianizing the
American People (1990); Cushing Strout, The New Heavens and New
Earth: Political Religion in America (1974); Michael E. Smith, Religious
Activism: The Historical Record, 27 Wm. & Mary L. Rev. 1087 (1986).
98. Lemon, 403 U.S. at 623.
99. Alan Schwarz, No Imposition of Religion: The Establishment
Clause, 77 Yale L.J. 700–701 (1968).

Moreover, since funding only public schools places parents whose children attend parochial schools at a competitive disadvantage, they will tend to oppose legislation benefiting public schools.[100] Similarly, Christian groups may lobby for a Sunday closing law, believing that their religious obligation to abstain from work on Sundays places them at a disadvantage in the marketplace. Moreover, they may believe it is in their interest, and in the interest of nonreligious people, to vigorously oppose an exemption from the law for Sabbatarians, who might gain a competitive advantage from being open on Sundays. But if the exemption is denied, Sabbatarians will just as vigorously oppose enactment of the Sunday closing law.

In sum, religious antagonism in the political arena, though probably regrettable, is a fact of life in our pluralistic government system, and it cannot be either effectively suppressed or greatly diminished through judicial review under the Religion Clauses.

ENDORSEMENT

A recently developed approach interpreting the religion provisions, championed by Justice O'Connor, urges that violations of the Establishment Clause should depend on whether a "reasonable observer"[101] (or an "objective observer")[102] would perceive the challenged government action as an endorsement of religion. This precept seeks to ensure equal standing within "the political community" for adherents of all (or no) religious faiths.[103]

This approach has many attractive features. Its condemnation of discrimination against persons because of their religious beliefs has already been included within my thesis. More generally, its disapproval of government's acting in

100. Choper, 56 Calif. L. Rev. at 273–74; see also John E. Nowak & Ronald D. Rotunda, Constitutional Law 1194 (4th ed. 1991).

101. Allegheny County, 492 U.S. at 635 (O'Connor J., concurring).

102. Jaffree, 472 U.S. at 76 (O'Connor, J., concurring).

103. Lynch v. Donnelly, 465 U.S. 668, 688 (1984) (O'Connor, J., concurring).

ways that offend or alienate citizens by making them feel like outsiders has a similar appeal to our humane instincts. At an operational level, it sidesteps one of the major disadvantages of the neutrality approach by permitting government accommodations for both minority and mainstream religions; it reasons that merely lifting special burdens that generally applicable regulations impose on members of some faiths does not "endorse" those religions, nor does it make members of the nonbenefited religions feel they have been disparaged because of their faith.[104]

A number of troublesome questions have arisen, however. One that has properly been given significant attention concerns how to define that "reasonable (or objective) observer," the hypothetical person who obviously plays a key role in the process. On the one hand, if this individual is a member of the religious or political mainstream, there is too great a risk that the perspective "will be inadequately sensitive to the impact of government actions on religious minorities, thereby in effect basing the protection of religious minorities on the judgment of the very majority that is accused of infringing the minority's religious autonomy."[105] On the other hand, if the perspective that determines the validity of government action turns on "the message received *by the minority or nonadherent*,"[106] this would grant something that I find too close to a self-interested veto for the minority and, as will be illustrated shortly, too restrictive of government accommodations that seek to promote religious liberty.[107]

Problems of definition, however, are surely not peculiar to any one approach.[108] Nor are they usually insoluble, especially if something short of a perfect answer is admissible. An

---

104. Amos, 483 U.S. at 349 (O'Connor, J., concurring).

105. Note, Developments—Religion and the State, 100 Harv. L. Rev. 1606, 1648 (1987).

106. Id.

107. See id. at 1650.

108. Compare the opinions of Justices Kennedy and O'Connor on the scope of the endorsement test in Allegheny County, 492 U.S. at 623 and 655.

effective solution here would be to entrust this "perspective-dependent"[109] inquiry to an independent judiciary whose great obligation is to secure the constitutional rights of those unable to rely on the political process. Although justices of the Supreme Court "cannot become someone else,"[110] they should, with their own solicitude for the values of religious liberty, either assume the view of a reasonable member of the political community who is faithful to the Constitution's protection of individual rights or ask whether a *reasonable minority observer,* who would be "acquainted with the text, legislative history, and implementation of the [challenged state action],"[111] *should feel* less than a full member of the political community.[112]

Other disadvantages of Justice O'Connor's thesis present more serious problems. The greatest difficulty, to me, is that reasonable perceptions of state approval or endorsement and legitimate feelings of alienation or offense by a segment of the population—and nothing more—trigger a holding of unconstitutionality.

It is, of course, iniquitous for government to intentionally deprecate a religious group. Realistically, in virtually all of the rare instances when this may occur, it will fail the Free Exercise Clause principle that I have sketched earlier and will develop in chapter 2. Theoretically, however, it will not rise to the level of a judicially enforceable constitutional violation in the highly unlikely case in which there are no adverse consequences beyond distressed sensibilities affecting the religious minority. It does not diminish the reprehensibility of the assumed government action to conserve scarce judicial resources for those occasions when they are more urgently

109. Note, 100 Harv. L. Rev. at 1647.
110. Mark Tushnet, "Of Church and State and the Supreme Court": Kurland Revisited, 1989 Sup. Ct. Rev. 373, 400.
111. Jaffree, 472 U.S. at 76 (O'Connor, J., concurring).
112. Although this process is basically normative rather than empirical, the Court's judgment should obviously be influenced by the perception (if fairly discernible) of "average" members of minority religious faiths and should be more strongly affected if their response is very widely shared.

needed.[113] This husbanding of capital is especially appropriate when the opposite rule, as we shall see shortly, would
substantially disable state attempts to respond to felt needs
of adherents of mainstream religious groups and to relieve
legally imposed burdens that prevent members of minority
faiths from pursuing their religious duties.

Most government action that alienates or offends people
because it is seen as approving or endorsing religion is not
the product of a deliberate government effort to be pejorative
toward those who are aggrieved. Rather, it results from the
adoption of well-meaning, legitimate, and sometimes even
successful attempts to improve the conditions of society. In
our pluralistic culture, "not all beliefs can achieve recognition
and ratification in the nation's laws and public policies; and
those whose positions are not so favored will sometimes feel
like 'outsiders.'"[114] It is clear that the Constitution cannot
generally provide relief when this occurs. The question then
is whether the Religion Clauses ought to spark judicial intervention when the alienated person contends that the offensive government action has not been employed to achieve
concededly secular ends but has been undertaken for the
purpose of favoring religious interests. To put it more forcefully, laws that endorse (or approve, or prefer) some religion,
or religion generally, constitute an important symbol in the
relationship between the state and its citizens. Moreover, they
confront a set of specific constitutional provisions that bear
on the matter. As a consequence, these government regulations are vulnerable on grounds of legitimacy, if not automatically void; they should certainly be invalid if they also produce the untoward feelings described.

Although I do not find this argument unpersuasive, I do

113. See Choper, Judicial Review and the National Political Process at
49, 169–70.
114. Steven D. Smith, Symbols, Perceptions, and Doctrinal Illusions:
Establishment Neutrality and the "No Endorsement" Test, 86 Mich. L. Rev.
266, 313 (1987); see also Mark Tushnet, The Constitution of Religion, 18
Conn. L. Rev. 701, 712 (1986): "[N]onadherents who believe that they are
excluded from the political community are merely expressing the disap-
pointment felt by everyone who has lost a fair fight in the arena of politics."

ultimately reject it. In my view, attempts by government to accommodate *either minority or mainstream* religions are often (indeed, usually) benign, genuine, and sometimes even important.[115] These efforts should be upheld even though they may be fairly seen as endorsing or approving religion and even though they may cause reasonable people to feel offended or alienated, as long as there is no proven threat of tangible danger to religious liberty beyond the speculation that "symbolic acts that seem inconsequential might, cumulatively or over time, foster an atmosphere of public discourse in which adherence to religion does make a difference."[116] A portion of the citizenry may feel like "outsiders," but "such endorsements do not appear to alter anyone's actual political standing in any realistic sense; no one loses the right to vote, the freedom to speak, or any other state or federal right if he or she does not happen to share the religious ideas that such practices appear to approve."[117] Moreover, although I would not contend that Article III's "concrete injury" requirement[118] precludes judicial enforcement of this approach to interpreting the Establishment Clause, still this feature of the endorsement test does run counter to the general precept that federal judicial power should not be invoked to remedy harm no greater than "indignation,"[119] "offense,"[120] or the "psychological consequence presumably produced by obser-

115. "Without indicating any view either as to religion's truthfulness or as to its value to society generally, government might acknowledge that many individual citizens care deeply about religion and that the religious concerns of such citizens merit respect and accommodation by government. This limited form of implicit approval or support might be described as 'accommodation endorsement.'" Smith, 86 Mich. L. Rev. at 277.

116. Neal R. Feigenson, Political Standing and Government Endorsement of Religion: An Alternative to Current Establishment Clause Doctrine, 40 De Paul L. Rev. 53, 81 (1990). But cf. Timothy Bakken, Religious Conversion and Social Evolution Clarified: Similarities between Traditional and Alternative Groups, 16 Small Group Behavior 157 (1985) (arguing that conversion is caused by psychological pressures rather than rational selection from a marketplace of ideas).

117. Smith, 86 Mich. L. Rev. at 307.

118. See United States v. Richardson, 418 U.S. 166, 177 (1974).

119. Harris v. City of Zion, 927 F.2d 1401, 1405 (7th Cir. 1991).

120. ACLU v. City of St. Charles, 794 F.2d 265 (7th Cir. 1986).

vation of conduct with which one disagrees."[121] Thus, under my thesis, Congress's making "In God We Trust" our national motto, or a city's using a Latin cross on its official seal,[122] would probably pass muster even though they express "an unambiguous choice"[123] in favor of theism and Christianity, respectively.

Several examples, covering a range of contexts, should indicate that the endorsement approach, fairly applied, is unduly restrictive of government authority. When the state includes religious groups within a category receiving a government benefit, even a very modest one such as the right of student organizations to meet in public school classrooms during noninstructional time, this may reasonably be viewed as government endorsement, as when a student religious club is permitted to use the premises to pray and to inculcate the tenets of the faith.[124] Despite the fact that the category may be large and open-ended, such as any group that contributes to the "intellectual, physical or social development of the student,"[125] and even though school officials may be committed to a course of impartiality,[126] it is clear that there are some groups (say, those committed to experimentation with drugs, or the study of erotica, or the rejection of parental authority) that will not be approved. Although some persons may fairly perceive the school's allowing the religious use as no more than indifference or neutrality on the part of school authori-

121. Valley Forge Christian College v. Americans United for Separation of Church and State, Inc., 454 U.S. 464, 485 (1982). See also Freedom from Religion Foundation v. Zielke, 845 F.2d 1463, 1467–68 (7th Cir. 1988) ("psychological harm" not adequate injury).

122. Harris v. City of Zion, 927 F.2d 1401 (7th Cir. 1991).

123. Id. at 1412.

124. See Board of Education v. Mergens, 496 U.S. 226 (1990).

125. Bender v. Williamsport Area School District, 741 F.2d 538, 548 (3d Cir. 1984) (quoting statement by school official), rev'd, 475 U.S. 534 (1986).

126. But see Michael L. Commons & Joseph A. Rodriguez, "Equal Access" without "Establishing" Religion: The Necessity for Assessing Social Perspective-Taking Skills and Institutional Atmosphere, 10 Develop. Rev. 323, 334 (1990) (presenting empirical data that casts doubt on the ability of secondary school administrators to treat all student groups equally).

ties in respect to "nonharmful" activities,[127] other credible observers may plausibly find it "inevitable that a public high school 'endorses' a religious club, in a common-sense use of the term, if the club happens to be one of many activities that the school permits students to choose in order to further the development of their intellect and character in an extra-curricular setting."[128]

When the state exempts a minority religion from a generally applicable prohibition, such as by permitting members of Native American religious groups to use peyote as part of their rituals,[129] this may reasonably be viewed as government endorsement of religion.[130] It may be a particularly fair perception by nonadherents who are criminally prosecuted for using peyote; they may justifiably feel alienated, offended, and placed outside the core of the political community when told that the defense for Native American religionists is not available to them. The distress is probably even more understandable when the legislative exception favors a mainstream religion, for example, excusing church-operated schools from the obligation of collective bargaining with unions representing lay faculty members.[131] An equally dramatic reaction of this kind might be expected from employee-members of a religious organization who, after being dismissed from their weekday secretarial or janitorial jobs for failing to be sufficiently devout on Sunday, learn that the church is exempt

127. See Douglas Laycock, Equal Access and Moments of Silence: The Equal Status of Religious Speech by Private Speakers, 81 Nw. U. L. Rev. 1, 14–20 (1986).

128. Mergens, 496 U.S. at 261 (Kennedy, J., concurring).

129. See Employment Division v. Smith, 494 U.S. 872 (1990).

130. See Tushnet, 1989 Sup. Ct. Rev. at 395 n. 73, who points out that accommodations of the kind being discussed "use religion as a basis for government classification, and they do so in the strongest sense of intentionally, that is, precisely in order to confer a benefit on some religions that does not flow either to nonbelievers or to all religions. The relevant question would then appear to be, what is the signal . . . sent by these accommodations? It is difficult to avoid the conclusion that permissible accommodations, with their necessarily disparate impact, indicate some degree of government approval of the practices that benefit from the accommodations."

131. See NLRB v. Catholic Bishop of Chicago, 440 U.S. 490 (1979).

from the national bar against religious discrimination in employment and that they therefore are remediless.[132] Along with many other "reasonable observers," these persons may appropriately sense that they are less than full-fledged beneficiaries of the government system.[133]

Finally, it seems clear that no stigmatizing of any person's beliefs is intended by government action, pursuant to the sentiments of America's mainstream religions, proclaiming a national day of thanksgiving to God.[134] (Indeed, this might even be called a *holi*day.) But it seems equally plain that the criteria for unconstitutionality under the endorsement approach are met.[135]

132. See Corporation of the Presiding Bishop v. Amos, 483 U.S. 327 (1987).

133. Justice O'Connor has attempted to avoid this problem by urging that, in assessing the validity of a government accommodation, "courts should assume that the 'objective observer' is acquainted with the Free Exercise Clause and the values it promotes. Thus individual perceptions, or resentment that a religious observer is exempted from a particular government requirement, would be entitled to little weight if the Free Exercise Clause strongly supported the exemption." Jaffree, 472 U.S. at 83 (O'Connor, J., concurring). A major difficulty with this rationale, apart from its potential circularity, is that in permitting only religious exemptions that are "strongly supported" by the Free Exercise Clause, it does not authorize voluntary legislative actions in furtherance of religious interests that are genuine but, for sundry doctrinal reasons, do not rise to (or come close to) the level of being constitutionally compelled. Of course, this part of the endorsement theory's approval of religious accommodations loses almost all of its force under the current rule that there are virtually no exemptions "strongly supported" by the Free Exercise Clause. See pp. 54–57 below.

134. "A favorable statement about one class is not necessarily a correlative pejorative remark about another class." William P. Marshall, The Concept of Offensiveness in Establishment and Free Exercise Jurisprudence, 66 Ind. L.J. 351, 365 (1991).

135. There are, of course, a number of other theories for resolving disputes under the Religion Clauses. These include the Court's well-known three-part "*Lemon*" test, see Lemon v. Kurtzman, 403 U.S. 602 (1971), for determining the scope of the Establishment Clause; widely discredited, it will be discussed at some length in chapter 5. The contours of Justice Kennedy's "coercion" approach—unfortunately titled, in my view; see Jesse H. Choper, Separation of Church and State: "New" Directions by the "New" Supreme Court, 34 J. Ch. & State 363, 364 (1992)—are probably not yet amplified enough to be helpfully considered; in any event, since its basic thrust appears to come quite close to my thesis, it will be reviewed indirectly throughout the book.

PREVIEW AND SYNOPSIS

The core of my proposed thesis for the Constitution's Religion Clauses and the variant ways these provisions seek to protect the fundamental value of religious liberty have now been sketched. The rest of this book will elaborate four basic principles analyzing the intent (or purpose) and impact (or effect) of government action that involves religion. The first two principles describe the function of the Free Exercise Clause, and the third and fourth concern the Establishment Clause. The four principles will vary in respect to the degree of detail needed for understanding, the amount of controversy expected to be engendered, and the level of complexity required for their explication. In the main, I believe that the weight of these factors (especially the last two) will increase progressively with the development of each succeeding principle.

OUTLINE OF PROPOSED PRINCIPLES

The "deliberate disadvantage" principle (chap. 2) almost always invalidates government action that intentionally handicaps people because of their religious beliefs. In an effort to afford greater security for religious freedom, the "burdensome effect" principle (chap. 3) requires a special exemption when generally applicable rules adversely affect the exercise of religious practices, but only in narrowly delineated circumstances. In contrast, the "intentional advantage" principle (chap. 4) generally permits the government to act in favor of religious interests, providing breathing room for the accommodation of both minority and mainstream religions but demanding that this be done nondiscriminatorily and without endangering religious liberty. Finally, the "independent impact" principle (chap. 5) forbids government programs that support religion but have no independent secular effect (a result that is achieved regardless of any benefit to religion), even though they provide advantages for sectarian interests as part of a broader classification.

EFFECT ON CURRENT DOCTRINE

Although adopting these principles would not require wholesale overthrowing of venerable judicial precedents or ingrained societal practices, their consistent application by the Court would result in some substantial modifications of existing doctrines and customs. For example, in regard to religion in the public schools, the current prohibitions of the Establishment Clause against vocal prayer and Bible reading,[136] religious invocations at graduation,[137] and on-premises released time programs[138] would remain, as would the mandate for equal access by religious groups to public school forums[139] and other property during noninstructional hours.[140] In contrast, the Court's decisions invalidating posting the Ten Commandments in public school classrooms,[141] excluding courses in evolution,[142] and including teaching of creation science[143] would have to be changed, as would the interdiction of moments for silent prayer.[144] Last, the Court's interpretation permitting off-premises released time plans[145] would be reversed. Similarly, most of the major rulings involving official acknowledgment of religion, such as Sunday closing laws[146] and displays of religious symbols during holiday seasons,[147] would be preserved. But the Court's uphold-

136. Abington School District v. Schempp, 374 U.S. 203 (1963); Engel v. Vitale, 370 U.S. 421 (1962).

137. Lee v. Weisman, 112 S.Ct. 2649 (1992).

138. McCollum v. Board of Education, 333 U.S. 203 (1948).

139. Widmar v. Vincent, 454 U.S. 263 (1981).

140. Board of Education v. Mergens, 496 U.S. 226 (1990); Lamb's Chapel v. Center Moriches Union Free School District, 113 S.Ct. 2141 (1993).

141. Stone v. Graham, 449 U.S. 39 (1980).

142. Epperson v. Arkansas, 393 U.S. 97 (1968).

143. Edwards v. Aguillard, 482 U.S. 578 (1987).

144. Wallace v. Jaffree, 472 U.S. 38 (1985). The thrust of this decision, however, is limited almost to its peculiar facts, and in my view most such programs will be upheld in the future even under present doctrine. See 54 U.S. Law Week 2196–97 (1985).

145. Zorach v. Clausen, 343 U.S. 306 (1952).

146. McGowan v. Maryland, 366 U.S. 420 (1961).

147. Allegheny County v. ACLU, 492 U.S. 573 (1989); Lynch v. Donnelly, 465 U.S. 668 (1984).

ing paid legislative chaplains[148] would be rejected, while its bar of a Christmas crèche in a county courthouse[149] would likely be overturned.

As for the matter of public financial assistance to church-related institutions, although a number of decisions beginning with *Lemon v. Kurtzman*[150] invalidating various programs of aid to elementary and secondary parochial schools[151] would be resolved differently,[152] the rationale of these opinions has already been severely undercut by more recent rulings[153] that are consistent with my view. Nevertheless, several major alterations would occur, probably the most controversial being the negation of *Walz v. Tax Commission*,[154] which allowed tax exemptions for property used exclusively for religious purposes, and the Court's approval of state payment (as part of a general program) to educate persons for their pursuit of a religious vocation.[155]

The justices' universally acknowledged precept under the Free Exercise Clause, forbidding government to single out one or more religions for adverse treatment,[156] would continue, but the Court's current approach of not ordinarily re-

148. Marsh v. Chambers, 463 U.S. 783 (1983).

149. Allegheny County v. ACLU, 492 U.S. 573 (1989).

150. 403 U.S. 602 (1971).

151. See, e.g., Committee for Public Education v. Nyquist, 413 U.S. 756 (1973); Meek v. Pittenger, 421 U.S. 349 (1975); Wolman v. Walter, 433 U.S. 229 (1977); Grand Rapids School District v. Ball, 473 U.S. 373 (1985); Aguilar v. Felton, 473 U.S. 402 (1985).

152. The Court's decisions upholding similar support for church-related institutions of higher education, e.g., Tilton v. Richardson, 403 U.S. 672 (1971); Roemer v. Maryland Public Works Board, 426 U.S. 736 (1976), would remain intact.

153. See, e.g., Mueller v. Allen, 463 U.S. 388 (1983); Zobrest v. Catalina Foothills School District, 113 S.Ct. 2462 (1993). See also Bowen v. Kendrick, 487 U.S. 589, 624–25 (1988) (Kennedy, J., concurring); Board of Education of Kiryas Joel Village School District v. Grumet, 114 S. Ct. 2481 (1984). See generally Choper, 34 J. Ch. & State at 368–71; 62 U.S. Law Week 2266 (1993); 63 U.S. Law Week 2233 (1994).

154. 397 U.S. 664 (1970).

155. Witters v. Washington Department of Services, 474 U.S. 481 (1986).

156. See, e.g. Torcaso v. Watkins, 367 U.S. 488 (1961); Church of the Lukumi Babalu Aye, Inc. v. City of Hialeah, 113 S.Ct. 2217 (1993).

quiring a religious exemption from generally applicable regulations that impose special burdens because of a faith's
particular tenets[157] would be abandoned. Still, this would simply constitute a return to the previous position that had been
in place for more than a generation.[158] Finally, the Court's
basic approval of government accommodations for religious
practices[159] would be maintained, although my thesis would
produce some results that would be more permissive[160] and
some that would be more restrictive[161] than the Court's decisions.

A NOTE ON STARE DECISIS

Extended consideration of the proper role of stare decisis
in constitutional adjudication is obviously beyond the scope
of this book. Still, several observations on the traditional justi-
fications for departing from precedent may be illuminating.
First, there does not appear to be any special reliance interest,[162] as occurs most forcefully in the commercial context,
on most constitutional rules in the church-state area. Second,
in contrast to the "intensely divisive" controversies surrounding the issues of abortion, racial segregation, and economic due process,[163] the details of the doctrines concerning
the Religion Clauses are by no means "deeply rooted in our
constitutional culture."[164] Indeed, the existing state of governing legal standards is both greatly in flux and riddled with
major defects and inconsistencies. The former condition may
be illustrated most generally by the continued expression of

157. Employment Division, Department of Human Resources v.
Smith, 494 U.S. 872 (1990).
158. This will be discussed in chapter 3.
159. See Corporation of the Presiding Bishop v. Amos, 483 U.S. 327
(1987).
160. See, e.g., Estate of Thornton v. Caldor, Inc., 472 U.S. 703 (1985).
161. See pp. 121–23 below.
162. See Burnet v. Coronado Oil & Gas Co., 285 U.S. 393, 405–13
(1932) (Brandeis, J., dissenting).
163. See Planned Parenthood of Southeastern Pennsylvania v. Casey,
112 S.Ct. 2791, 2812–14 (1992).
164. Id. at 2862 (Rehnquist, C.J., concurring in part and dissenting in
part).

dissatisfaction by varied justices with the Court's basic framework for resolution of problems under the Establishment Clause,[165] and more specifically by the Court's recent recasting of its primary approach to issues under the Free Exercise Clause.[166] As for the matter of doctrinal confusion, there are numerous examples that have pervaded the development of constitutional precepts under the Religion Clauses reaching back from the more than forty years of conflict between the Court's differing treatment of on-premises and off-premises released time[167] to the more recent difficulty in reconciling the Court's sustaining statutory exemptions for churches from property taxation[168] and employment discrimination laws,[169] on the one hand, and its invalidating a state's grant of a sales tax exemption for religious publications[170] on the other.[171] "At a certain point, when dissatisfaction with the

165. See, e.g., Lamb's Chapel, 113 S.Ct. at 2150 (Scalia, J., concurring): "I agree with the long list of constitutional scholars who have criticized *Lemon* and bemoaned the strange Establishment Clause geometry of crooked lines and wavering shapes its intermittent use has produced"; Allegheny County, 492 U.S. at 655–56 (Kennedy, J., concurring in part and dissenting in part): "Persuasive criticism of [the] *Lemon* [test] has emerged. See Edwards v. Aguillard, 482 U.S. 578, 636–640 (1987) (Scalia, J., dissenting); Aguilar v. Felton, 473 U.S. 402, 426–430 (1985) (O'Connor, J., dissenting); Wallace v. Jaffree, 472 U.S. 38, 108–113 (1985) (Rehnquist, J., dissenting); Roemer v. Maryland Board of Public Works, 426 U.S. 736, 768–769 (1976) (White, J., concurring in judgment). Our cases often question its utility in providing concrete answers to Establishment Clause questions, calling it but a " 'helpful signpos[t]' " or ' "guidelin[e]," ' to assist our deliberations rather than a comprehensive test. Mueller v. Allen, 463 U.S. 388, 394 (1983) . . . ; see Lynch v. Donnelly, 465 U.S. 668, 679 (1984) ('we have repeatedly emphasized our unwillingness to be confined to any single test or criterion in this sensitive area'). Substantial revision of our Establishment Clause doctrine may be in order."

166. Employment Division, Department of Human Resources v. Smith, 494 U.S. 872 (1990). See also Church of the Lukumi Babalu Aye, 113 S.Ct. at 2240 (Souter, J., concurring) ("the Court should re-examine the rule *Smith* declared").

167. See text at notes 138 and 145 above.

168. Walz v. Tax Commission, 397 U.S. 664 (1970).

169. Corporation of the Presiding Bishop v. Amos, 483 U.S. 327 (1987).

170. Texas Monthly, Inc. v. Bullock, 489 U.S. 1 (1989).

171. As for the "conceptual disaster area" forged in respect to aid to parochial schools, see chapter 5.

status quo reaches a sufficient magnitude, we can expect to see the doctrinal chain snapped."[172] Indeed, adopting a coherent set of principles in this area, rather than being at war with the prescription of stare decisis, would actually advance the values of a society committed to being governed by the rule of law.

172. Post, Theories of Constitutional Interpretation at 27.

2

....

Deliberate Disadvantage Principle

Government action that intentionally prejudices individuals because they have or do not have certain religious beliefs should be held to violate the Free Exercise Clause unless the government demonstrates that the regulation is necessary to a compelling interest.

As already noted, the precept of religious equality has been indisputably and consistently recognized by the Supreme Court[1] and "receives overwhelming support in the American tradition of church and state."[2] It closely parallels the core prohibition in the Equal Protection Clause of the Fourteenth Amendment against invidious racial discrimination, and its logical and normative underpinnings extend to government's acting hostilely toward persons because they are nonbelievers as well as to those who are prejudiced because they are of a particular religious faith.

1. See, e.g., Everson v. Board of Education, 330 U.S. 1, 15 (1947) for the bedrock articulation. Although conceding that religious discrimination "is inextricably connected with the continuing vitality of the Free Exercise Clause," Larson v. Valente, 456 U.S. 228, 245 (1982), the Court has regularly invoked the Establishment Clause as the source of the prohibition. Id.; Gillette v. United States, 401 U.S. 437 (1971); Everson. As I noted earlier, there is no inherently persuasive reason to employ one of the Religion Clauses rather than the other to secure a particular aspect of religious liberty. But as I have discussed at greater length elsewhere, see Jesse H. Choper, The Free Exercise Clause: A Structural Overview and an Appraisal of Recent Developments, 27 Wm. & Mary L. Rev. 943, 957–61 (1986), both functional and formal considerations make the Free Exercise Clause preferable for the task at hand.

2. Arlin M. Adams & Charles J. Emmerich, A Heritage of Religious Liberty, 137 U. Pa. L. Rev. 1559, 1636 (1989).

Resemblance to Race

There are powerful similarities between government's singling out persons for imposition of adverse consequences either because of their skin color or because of their ideological beliefs, and these likenesses call for analogous handling under the Constitution. Perhaps the strongest justification for strict judicial scrutiny of any official attempt to accord persons less than equal respect and dignity because of their religious beliefs or race rests in the fact that both throughout history and during more recent times, efforts to do so have been similarly rooted in "hate, prejudice, vengeance, [and] hostility."[3] Although race may seem to be a more immutable condition than religion,[4] and though religious belief systems may appear to have a more interwoven effect than race on the conduct of people's lives, both traits have been the strikingly similar objects of public (and private) stereotyping, stigma, subordination, and persecution. In response, the Court has properly viewed racial and religious discriminations with particular suspicion[5] and demanded that "they be justified in terms of a significantly more pressing governmental objective than normally required, and a near perfect fit between the characterizations employed and the objective pursued."[6] This

3. Joseph Tussman & Jacobus tenBroek, The Equal Protection of the Laws, 37 Calif. L. Rev. 341, 358 (1949).

4. For discussion of the immutability of religious beliefs, see Timothy L. Hall, Religion, Equality, and Difference, 65 Temp. L. Rev. 1, 62–63 (1992).

5. In New Orleans v. Dukes, 427 U.S. 297, 303 (1976), the Court unanimously categorized both religion and race as "suspect" classifications.

6. Hall, 65 Temp. L. Rev. at 55. The few decisions of the Supreme Court that have involved deliberate disfavoring of persons or groups because of religious beliefs they do or do not hold have, as urged here, employed the test of strict scrutiny either expressly or implicitly to invalidate the regulations. See Church of the Lukumi Babalu Aye, Inc. v. City of Hialeah, 113 S.Ct. 2217 (1993) (city forbade ritual animal sacrifice); McDaniel v. Paty, 435 U.S. 618 (1978) (state disqualified members of clergy from being legislators); Torcaso v. Watkins, 367 U.S. 448 (1961) (state required notaries public to take oath of belief in God); Larson v. Valente, 456 U.S. 228 (1982) (state imposed registration and reporting requirements only upon religious organizations that solicit more than half their funds from nonmembers). The one possible exception, Gillette v. United States, 401

method is a "way of uncovering official attempts to inflict inequality for its own sake—to treat a group worse not in the service of some overriding social goal but largely for the sake of simply disadvantaging its members,"[7] a course of conduct based on assumptions of the "differential worth"[8] of religious and racial groups, including judgments of their odiousness or inferiority. Since judicial decisions make it extremely difficult for these stringent criteria to be met either factually[9] or legally,[10] very few classifications that intentionally prejudice persons because of their race or religion have been or will be upheld.[11]

It is important to note the peculiar nature of the personal quality or characteristic that is the subject of the special judicial protection of the "deliberate disadvantage" principle: at

---

U.S. 437 (1971), did not acknowledge as discriminatory the Selective Service Act provision that exempted from the draft individuals who were religiously opposed to "war in any form" but did not excuse those who were religiously opposed only to "unjust wars." In any event, the Court's reasoning in *Gillette* is not necessarily inconsistent with its usual approach to the problem. See Choper, 27 Wm. & Mary L. Rev. at 960.

7. John Hart Ely, Democracy and Distrust 153 (1980).

8. Paul Brest, In Defense of the Antidiscrimination Principle, 90 Harv. L. Rev. 1, 7 (1976).

9. See Korematsu v. United States, 323 U.S. 214 (1944) and Hirabayashi v. United States, 320 U.S. 81 (1943) (upholding military orders for exclusion and curfew of Japanese Americans on the West Coast during World War II); cf. Lee v. Washington, 390 U.S. 333, 334 (1968) (concurring opinion of Black, Harlan, and Stewart, JJ.) (discussing the possibility of temporary racial segregation in prison in response to racial tensions that threaten prison security).

10. The Court has ruled that government action preferring racial minorities and disfavoring the racial majority may be permissible, e.g., to remedy past discrimination in violation of statutes or the Equal Protection Clause. City of Richmond v. J. A. Croson Co., 488 U.S. 469 (1989); Sheet Metal Workers' Local 28 v. EEOC, 478 U.S. 421 (1986). Similarly, as has already been suggested, and as will be developed in chapters 3 and 4, my thesis authorizes preferring religious interests under certain conditions. And as will be developed in chapter 5, it also requires that religious groups sometimes be disfavored in order to satisfy the values of the Establishment Clause.

11. Query as to the validity of requiring immunization of all members of a racial or religious group that seems peculiarly susceptible to a particular illness such as sickle-cell anemia or Tay-Sachs disease.

issue are beliefs or membership in a group that shares a set of beliefs, rather than participation in some course of generally regulated conduct. This concerns an ideal that extends beyond the value of religious liberty—one that is deeply ingrained in several constitutional provisions apart from the Religion Clauses. For example, the deliberate disadvantage principle could just as readily be grounded in the First Amendment freedoms of speech and association, which have frequently been used to protect a broad range of ideological convictions including religion;[12] as a consequence, the principle requires no judicial definition of "religion."

Inquiry into Motive

The deliberate disadvantage principle plainly applies to government regulations that discriminate on their face. But it also condemns more subtle forms of state action that, by their explicit language, may appear to accomplish a constitutionally permissible end but whose real aim is to prejudice persons because they hold or do not hold certain religious convictions. This requires the Court to ascertain whether the lawmaking body intended to achieve a goal through the effect of the regulation that is not plainly prescribed by its words.

NARROW SCOPE

From its early efforts to the present time, the Court's approach to the Religion Clauses, in contrast to almost all other areas of constitutional adjudication, has made legislative and administrative motivation a major criterion.[13] There

12. See Jesse H. Choper, Defining "Religion" in the First Amendment, 1982 U. Ill. L. Rev. 579, 581–83, also suggesting the "fundamental rights branch of equal protection doctrine" as a source of protection against "government action that deliberately singles out one or more religious groups for adverse treatment or that penalizes or withholds benefits from persons because of their peculiar sectarian beliefs."

13. See McDaniel, 435 U.S. at 636 n. 9 (Brennan, J., concurring): "In contrast to the general rule that legislative motive or purpose is not a relevant inquiry in determining the constitutionality of a statute, our cases under the Religion Clauses have uniformly held such an inquiry necessary."

is broad agreement, reaching back to the landmark ruling in *Fletcher v. Peck*,[14] that divining the real motive of lawmakers "is a perilous enterprise"[15] and "a notoriously tricky affair."[16] Thus it is important to emphasize the very limited scope of this delicate judicial task required by the deliberate disadvantage principle.

First, there is a substantial "distinction between those things a legislator hopes to accomplish *by the operation of the statute* for which he is voting, and those things he hopes personally to achieve *by the act of his vote*."[17] The deliberate disadvantage principle concerns only "hopes" in the former category. For example, in *Edwards v. Aguillard,* the Court had before it a Louisiana statute that forbade "the teaching of the theory of evolution in public schools unless accompanied by instruction in 'creation science.'"[18] The former category of "hopes" includes the question whether a legislator "voted for the Act. . .because he wanted to foster religion or because he wanted to improve education."[19] In contrast, the kinds of "hopes" described at length by Justice Scalia's dissenting opinion in *Edwards* fall more readily into the latter category: a legislator "may have thought the bill would provide jobs for his district, or may have wanted to make amends with a faction of his party he had alienated on another vote, or he may have been a close friend of the bill's sponsor, or he may have been repaying a favor he owed the Majority Leader, or he may have hoped the Governor would appreciate his vote and make a fundraising appearance for him, or he may have been pressured to vote for a bill he disliked by a wealthy

14. 10 U.S. (6 Cranch) 87, 130 (1810).
15. Thomas A. Schweitzer, Lee v. Weisman and the Establishment Clause: Are Invocations and Benedictions at Public School Graduation Constitutionally Unspeakable? 69 U. Det. Mercy L. Rev. 113, 192 (1992).
16. Hall, 65 Temp. L. Rev. at 65.
17. John Hart Ely, Legislative and Administrative Motivation in Constitutional Law, 79 Yale L.J. 1205, 1218 (1970) (discussing Ira Michael Heyman, The Chief Justice, Racial Segregation, and the Friendly Critics, 49 Calif. L. Rev. 104 [1961]).
18. 482 U.S. 578 (1987).
19. Id. at 637 (Scalia, J., dissenting).

contributor or by a flood of constituent mail, or he may have
been seeking favorable publicity, or he may have been reluc-
tant to hurt the feelings of a loyal staff member who worked
on the bill, or he may have been settling an old score with a
legislator who opposed the bill, or he may have been mad at
his wife who opposed the bill, . . . or, of course, he may have
had (and very likely did have) a combination of some of the
above and many other motivations."[20] Admittedly, there is
only a difference of degree rather than kind "between those
things a person intends to result immediately from his act [the
former category], and other more distant and less certain, but
nonetheless intended, results [the latter category]."[21] Moreover, resolving even questions in the former category "demands a sensitive inquiry into such circumstantial and direct
evidence of intent as may be available."[22] But as we shall
see, it appears to be within the judiciary's capacity to reach a
decision about the former category with adequate certainty,
whereas exploring motivations in the latter category seems to
be "almost always an impossible task."[23]

Second, as analogously true with regard to forbidden racial discrimination under the Equal Protection Clause, the
only goal of examining legislative motive under the deliberate
disadvantage principle is to uncover whether the regulation
was meant to implement unspoken antagonism toward persons or groups because of their religious beliefs. This isolated
judicial inquiry is very narrow and is vastly different from
asking whether the legislators, responding in various inde-
finable ways to religious inspiration, sought in some oblique
fashion to "advance" religion when promulgating a regulation that is religiously neutral in both its language and its
administration. As we shall see in chapter 5, that effort generates difficulties that are acutely more complex. It is one thing
to question whether a lawmaking body acted with racial or

20. Id.
21. Ely, 79 Yale L.J. at 1219.
22. Village of Arlington Heights v. Metropolitan Housing Development Corp., 429 U.S. 252, 266 (1977).
23. Edwards v. Aguillard, 482 U.S. at 636 (Scalia, J., dissenting).

religious animus, that is, whether "an admittedly impermissible motive has poisoned the political process."[24] It is quite another to determine whether the purpose of a law that has concededly been enacted to serve permissible public welfare goals was in some part attributable to the religious background, aspirations, or beliefs (or other ideological tenets) of members of the legislature. "Beginning with the Founding itself, the history of the United States reveals an inseparable connection between religion, morality, and law. Many of our laws, even our basic system of constitutional government and individual rights, rest to a significant degree on religious understandings of the world, of human beings, and of social relationships."[25] Further, as observed in chapter 1, individuals and groups often support a wide variety of political/social/economic policies because of their religious ideals.[26] If the "real purpose" of programs of this kind were open to judicial probing, then laws against homicide and theft would be constitutionally vulnerable under the Religion Clauses.[27] Because "religious beliefs and values may permeate a person's world view by underlying, reinforcing, and interacting with other 'secular' convictions,"[28] many legislators themselves would find it impossible to "fathom their reactions to cross-currents of psychic stimuli"[29] so as to distinguish between which of their views of what is good or bad for society have a worldly

24. Hall, 65 Temp. L. Rev. at 66.

25. Daniel O. Conkle, Religious Purpose, Inerrancy, and the Establishment Clause, 67 Ind. L.J. 1, 6–7 (1991).

26. "Welfare programs may be supported for religious reasons relating to perceived obligations to the poor. Statutes restricting the availability of abortions may be supported by individuals who believe that abortion violates God's law. The Civil Rights Act of 1964 was passed with substantial support from religious believers who supported the Act, in part, on religious grounds." Hall, 65 Temp. L. Rev. at 68. See generally R. Kent Greenawalt, Religious Convictions and Political Choice (1988); Peter L. Benson & Dorothy L. Williams, Religion on Capitol Hill: Myths and Realities (1982).

27. See Steven D. Smith, Separation and the "Secular": Reconstructing the Disestablishment Decision, 67 Tex. L. Rev. 955, 998 (1989).

28. Schweitzer, 69 U. Det. Mercy L. Rev. at 195.

29. Gary C. Leedes, Taking the Bible Seriously, 1987 Am. Bar Found. Res. J. 311, 315.

basis and which have deep religious roots. The problems for judges in unscrambling the multiple purposes and unconscious motivations in this context are greatly exacerbated compared with those involved in the surgically precise inquiry under the Equal Protection Clause and deliberate disadvantage principle.

EXAMPLES

Fortunately, as recent experience has shown even with regard to intentional discrimination against racial and ethnic minorities, violations of the deliberate disadvantage principle should occur very infrequently,[30] and when one does its suspicious appearance will ordinarily be fairly clear, even if wrapped "in the verbal cellophane"[31] of legitimacy. A few examples enforcing the racial equality precept of the Fourteenth and Fifteenth Amendments should help demonstrate the usual ease by which the judiciary may state the obvious to smoke out the overwhelming majority of legislators' illicit purposes. In *Gomillion v. Lightfoot*,[32] the Court held that the gerrymandering of Tuskegee, Alabama, which altered the city's shape "from a square to an uncouth 28-sided figure," was unconstitutional because it could have no purpose other than the disfranchisement of blacks in municipal elections. The Court found it "difficult to appreciate what stands in the way of adjudging a statute having this inevitable effect invalid."[33] A similar case, *Guinn v. United States*,[34] dramatically

30. As to the rarity of deliberate government discrimination against people because they do or do not hold certain religious convictions, see note 6 above and the first sentence of the next paragraph.

31. United States v. Kahriger, 345 U.S. 22, 38 (1953) (Frankfurter, J., dissenting.)

32. 364 U.S. 339 (1960).

33. Id. at 342. "Fanciful suggestions might have been possible, and they might have included whim; but they would all have been disingenuous on their face given the meticulous care with which, running the line house-by-house, the legislature succeeded in [removing all but four or five of the municipality's black voters while] not eliminating a single previous white resident of Tuskegee from the new city limits." Alexander M. Bickel, The Least Dangerous Branch: The Supreme Court at the Bar of Politics 211 (1962).

34. 238 U.S. 347 (1915).

illustrates that some instances of "inevitable effect" "may for all practical purposes demonstrate unconstitutionality because in various circumstances the discrimination is very difficult to explain on nonracial grounds."[35] *Guinn* invalidated Oklahoma's literacy test for voting because its "grandfather clause" effectively exempted whites. Oklahoma then immediately enacted a new rule providing that all persons who had previously voted were qualified for life but that all others must register within a twelve-day period or be permanently disfranchised. In *Lane v. Wilson*,[36] the Court rejected this law on the ground that the Fifteenth Amendment "nullifies sophisticated as well as simple-minded modes of discrimination."[37]

Until recently there were no cases in which the Supreme Court had found it necessary to examine legislative motive in order to secure the religious liberty protected by the deliberate disadvantage principle. But this changed with the 1993 decision of *Church of the Lukumi Babalu Aye, Inc. v. City of Hialeah*,[38] invalidating ordinances that barred ritual animal sacrifice. Although the Court agreed that the words of the regulations were "consistent with the claim of facial discrimination,"[39] because the language was "not conclusive,"[40] the Court went on to find that "the record . . . compels the conclusion that suppression of . . . [religious] worship service was the object of the ordinances."[41] No member of the Court dissented from the following judgment: "The pattern . . . discloses animosity to Santeria adherents and their religious practices; the ordinances by their own terms target this religious exercise; the texts of the ordinances were gerrymandered with care to proscribe religious killings of animals but to exclude almost all secular killings; and the ordinances sup-

35. Washington v. Davis, 426 U.S. 229, 242 (1976).
36. 307 U.S. 268 (1939).
37. Id. at 275.
38. 113 S.Ct. 2217 (1993).
39. Id. at 2227.
40. Id.
41. Id.

press much more religious conduct than is necessary in order to achieve the legitimate ends asserted in their defense."[42]

Moreover, there has been a series of church-state rulings, involving government programs to *favor* religion,[43] that further demonstrates that finding a law's "pre-eminent purpose,"[44] as required to identify deliberate *disfavor*, should usually be a fairly straightforward task. In *Epperson v. Arkansas*,[45] invalidating a statute prohibiting the teaching of evolution in public schools, the Court concluded that "Arkansas' law selects from the body of knowledge a particular segment which it proscribes for the sole reason that it is deemed to conflict with a particular religious doctrine."[46] Citing newspaper advertisements and letters supporting adoption of the statute in 1938, the Court found it "clear that fundamentalist sectarian conviction was and is the law's reason for existence."[47] In *Torcaso v. Watkins*, the Court observed that there could be "no dispute about the [religious] purpose"[48] of a requirement that public officeholders declare a belief in God. And in *Engel v. Vitale*, the Court had "no doubt that . . . daily classroom invocation of God's blessings as prescribed in the Regents' prayer is a religious activity,"[49] a conclusion that was greatly bolstered by the Regents' Statement on Moral and Spiritual Training in the Schools, which proclaimed the prayer's goal to be "teaching our children . . . that Almighty God is their Creator, and that by Him they have been endowed with their inalienable rights."[50]

In other cases invalidating religious influences in the public schools, the Court has drawn on common understanding to impeach what it concluded were obviously implausible assertions that there were nonreligious purposes for the chal-

42. Id. at 2231.
43. See also pp. 98–99 below.
44. Stone v. Graham, 449 U.S. 39, 41–42 (1980).
45. 393 U.S. 97 (1968).
46. Id. at 103.
47. Id. at 107–8.
48. 367 U.S. 488, 489 (1961).
49. 370 U.S. 421, 424 (1962).
50. Id., Record p. 28.

lenged practices. In *Abington School District v. Schempp*,[51] the school boards contended that the reading, without comment, of a chapter of the Bible at the opening of the school day served such nonsectarian ends as promoting moral values, inspiring pupil tolerance and discipline, contradicting the materialistic trends of the times, and teaching literature. The Court's brusque reply was that "surely, the place of the Bible as an instrument of religion cannot be gainsaid."[52] In *Stone v. Graham*,[53] the Court summarily reversed a decision of the Kentucky Supreme Court that had upheld the practice of posting copies of the Ten Commandments in public school classrooms. The avowed purpose for the state program was printed at the bottom of each copy: "The secular application of the Ten Commandments is clearly seen in its adoption as the fundamental legal code of Western Civilization and the Common Law of the United States."[54] Observing that the Commandments were not integrated into any study of history, ethics, or comparative religion but could have only the effect, if any, of inducing students to meditate on, revere, or perhaps obey them, the Court quite peremptorily concluded that "the Ten Commandments are undeniably a sacred text in the Jewish and Christian faiths, and no legislative recitation of a supposed secular purpose can blind us to that fact."[55] In the late 1950s, when a New York school board similarly required that a nonsectarian version of the Ten Commandments be placed in all classrooms, it was not so disingenuous as the Kentucky legislature. The New York panel's announced purpose was "to strengthen the moral and spiritual values of the students in the school district."[56] Finally, in *Wallace v. Jaffree,* an Alabama statute authorizing a minute of silence in all public schools "for meditation" was amended to read "for meditation or voluntary prayer."[57] The only con-

51. 374 U.S. 203 (1963).
52. Id. at 224.
53. 449 U.S. 39 (1980).
54. Id. at 41.
55. Id.
56. Note, 22 Alb. L. Rev. 156 (1958).
57. 472 U.S. 38, 40 (1985).

ceivable purpose for the changed language was to clarify the intent that the period might be used for prayer. No state witnesses suggested otherwise, and the amendment's prime legislative sponsor acknowledged the aim of returning prayer to public schools.[58]

PROCEDURES FOR ASCERTAINMENT

The Court, aided by perceptive commentators,[59] has developed an approach for ascertaining invidious purpose in the area of race.[60] Although the deliberate disadvantage principle concerns a similar "hard-core" violation of fundamental constitutional values, the justices have been less clear on a detailed method for determining an illicit motive in the area of religion. Nonetheless, the parallels between race and religion just outlined strongly suggest that the same system be employed. Moreover, since generally applicable laws that impose *unintentional* burdens on persons because of their religious beliefs are not morally reprehensible and serve legitimate public policies, the second principle of my thesis, to be discussed in chapter 3, will propose that special exemptions from such laws be accorded religion only in very limited circumstances. Thus it is especially important to develop careful procedures to detect intentional religious discrimination when it exists.

Articulation of a detailed set of rules on the subject is beyond the scope of this book, but a few basic points may be sketched. The approach should *not* be that invalidity requires that "there was *no question* that the statute or activity was motivated *wholly* by religious considerations"[61] of the kind prohibited by the deliberate disadvantage principle. Such government action, "to avoid suspicion, must have more than a mere rational relationship to some valid nonreligious pur-

58. Id. at 56–57 & n. 43.
59. See, e.g., Paul Brest, Palmer v. Thompson: An Approach to the Problem of Unconstitutional Legislative Motive, 1971 Sup. Ct. Rev. 95.
60. See Village of Arlington Heights v. Metropolitan Housing Development Corp., 429 U.S. 252 (1977).
61. Lynch v. Donnelly, 465 U.S. 668, 680 (1984) (emphasis added).

pose";[62] it should be more than "minimally related to the promotion" of some permissible objective.[63] These extremely deferential standards would automatically immunize virtually all regulations, including the kind being considered, that would threaten religious liberty in the most objectionable way. If the Court has good reason to believe—and it may be that there is no "better" way to describe the "test,"which as we have seen is usually satisfied quite readily—that a deliberate effort to harm persons or groups because of their religious beliefs has played a material role in decision making, especially if the Court's judgment is informed by a general societal perception, then certain procedural rules should come into play. For example, in these circumstances, in order to dispel the inference of illicit motivation, I would favor placing the burden on the state to show that it has no alternative means to achieve its permissible (nonpunitive) objective "that is both less drastic in terms of effects adverse to the . . . [deliberate disadvantage principle] and not beyond the state's capacity to implement."[64] By stipulating that an improper purpose need be only a material (or substantial) rather than the predominant (or primary) factor in the legislative arena in order to trigger special attention, and by then assigning the ultimate burden of justification to those defending the government action rather than to those claiming that religious disadvantage was intended, this procedure seeks to uncover concealed animosity toward religious groups while also allowing the state to accomplish any lawful goal it may have.

62. Stanley Ingber, Religion or Ideology: A Needed Clarification of the Religion Clauses, 41 Stan. L. Rev. 233, 329 (1989).

63. Brest, 1971 Sup. Ct. Rev. at 122.

64. Gary J. Simson, The Establishment Clause in the Supreme Court: Rethinking the Court's Approach, 72 Corn. L. Rev. 905, 923 (1987).

3

....

Burdensome Effect Principle

If government regulations of conduct that are generally applicable and enacted for secular/neutral purposes (i.e., without intent to provide an advantage to religious interests or prejudice individuals because of their religious beliefs) conflict with action or inaction pursuant to the tenets of a particular religion, the Free Exercise Clause should be held to require an exemption under the following circumstances: the claimant has suffered cognizable injury; the exemption does not violate the Establishment Clause; the exemption does not require the government to abandon its entire regulatory program; the individual's beliefs are sincerely held; violation of those beliefs entails extratemporal consequences; an alternative burden is imposed if one exists that does not conflict with the religious objector's beliefs; and the government cannot demonstrate that denial of the exemption is necessary to a compelling interest.

EXISTING DOCTRINE AND ITS SHORTCOMINGS

CURRENT STATE OF CONSTITUTIONAL LAW

For more than a quarter century, between 1963 and 1990, the Supreme Court's basic doctrine in respect to the kind of government regulations just described was that their discriminatory *impact,* or disadvantageous *effect,* made them presumptively invalid under the Free Exercise Clause. This required that a religious exemption be granted unless the law survived what was essentially a test of "strict scrutiny": the state would have to show that the exemption undermined an overriding, substantial, compelling, or important interest that could not be achieved by some narrower alternative means.

This doctrine was abandoned in *Employment Division, Department of Human Resources v. Smith*,[1] which addressed the question whether the Free Exercise Clause required an exemption from Oregon's prohibition on possession of peyote as applied to its use for sacramental purposes at a ceremony of the Native American Church. The Court leaned heavily in the direction of the neutrality approach, discussed in chapter 1, by holding that the First Amendment does *not* bar "application of a neutral, generally applicable law to religiously motivated action."[2]

The *Smith* decision's analysis of precedent and policy has been widely criticized elsewhere,[3] prompting an unprecedented coalition of political forces and an extraordinary congressional reaction to be described below.[4] Most significant for our purposes is that, as I have already noted in the discussion of the shortcomings of the neutrality principle, the *Smith* approach is insufficiently protective of religious liberty. Virtually all possibilities for government accommodation of free exercise interests now depend completely on the political process, which must respond, for example, to the fact that "employment discrimination laws conflict with the Roman Catholic male priesthood; laws against serving alcoholic beverages to minors conflict with the celebration of communion; regulations requiring hard hats in construction areas can effectively exclude Amish and Sikhs from the workplace; practices of public hospitals can conflict with the religious scruples of doctors and nurses in such matters as euthanasia and abortion; zoning laws interfere with religious ministries; laws requiring jury service conflict with the tenets of Jehovah's Witnesses; laws giving historic preservation commissions authority over

1. 494 U.S. 872 (1990).
2. 494 U.S. at 881.
3. See, e.g., Jesse H. Choper, The Rise and Decline of the Constitutional Protection of Religious Liberty, 70 Neb. L. Rev. 651 (1991); Douglas Laycock, The Remnants of Free Exercise, 1990 Sup. Ct. Rev. 1; Michael W. McConnell, Free Exercise Revisionism and the Smith Decision, 57 U. Chi. L. Rev. 1109 (1990); James D. Gordon, Free Exercise on the Mountaintop, 79 Calif. L. Rev. 91 (1991).
4. See N.Y. Times, Nov. 17, 1993, sec. A, p. 18, col. 1.

changes in old buildings, if applied to churches, can result in official second-guessing of ecclesiastical decisions; and laws establishing the schedule of compulsory public schools conflict with the prayer requirements of Muslim students."[5] The Court itself admitted that entrusting free exercise interests to popularly elected representatives "may fairly be said . . . [to] place at a relative disadvantage those religious practices that are not widely engaged in."[6] Legislatures are highly imperfect protectors of individual constitutional rights. They can be careless, insensitive, or even overtly hostile to particular sectarian interests; they can be unaware of certain religious needs because a group is obscure or inadequately organized; or they may simply not have the time to consider a religious exemption request, all to the same effect.[7] As a consequence, there is too great a risk that minority faiths, left without judicial recourse when generally applicable government regulations threaten to infringe on their religious liberty, will be subjected to serious restrictions on their ability to follow their beliefs. Courts are also fallible, but judicial review at least provides a second chance to be heard.[8]

The problem is sharply illustrated by the facts of *Smith* itself. The members of the Native American Church believed in the use of peyote as a sacramental act, a crucial tenet of their faith. Moreover, as Justice Blackmun's dissenting opin-

5. Michael W. McConnell, Accommodation of Religion, 60 Geo. Wash. L. Rev. 685, 694 (1992).

6. 494 U.S. at 890.

7. Douglas Laycock, Formal, Substantive, and Disaggregated Neutrality toward Religion, 39 De Paul L. Rev. 993, 1015–16 (1990).

8. On whether a constitutional right of religious exemption was originally intended, compare Michael W. McConnell, The Origins and Historical Understanding of Free Exercise of Religion, 103 Harv. L. Rev. 1409 (1990) with Philip A. Hamburger, A Constitutional Right of Religious Exemption: An Historical Perspective, 60 Geo. Wash. L. Rev. 915 (1992). See also Kurt T. Lash, The Second Adoption of the Free Exercise Clause: Religious Exemptions under the Fourteenth Amendment, 88 Nw. U. L. Rev. 1106 (1994) (Privileges or Immunities Clause of Fourteenth Amendment incorporated a principle of religious exemption from generally applicable laws even though not originally intended by framers in 1791).

ion persuasively argued, the government's interest in criminal prohibition of religious peyote use was insignificant at best.[9] Indeed, at the time *Smith* was decided, Oregon itself had only once sought to prosecute for religious possession of peyote, and shortly after prevailing in the Supreme Court in *Smith*, the state decided to exempt sacramental use of the drug.[10] Further, it is difficult to reconcile a ban on the use of peyote by members of the Native American Church with the statutory exemption granted for the sacramental use of wine during Prohibition.[11] The fact is that "powerful and influential religions will usually receive adequate protection in the political arena. One rarely sees laws that force mainstream Protestants to violate their consciences. Judicially enforceable exemptions under the free exercise clause are therefore needed to ensure that unpopular or unfamiliar faiths will receive the same consideration afforded mainstream or generally respected religions by the representative branches."[12]

9. Justice Blackmun rejected each of the three interests that Oregon advanced as "compelling." First, as for "protecting the health and safety of its citizens from the dangers of unlawful drugs," Justice Blackmun responded: "The carefully circumscribed ritual context in which respondents used peyote is far removed from the irresponsible and unrestricted recreational use of unlawful drugs. The Native American Church's internal restrictions on, and supervision of, its members' use of peyote substantially obviate the State's health and safety concerns." 494 U.S. at 911, 913 (Blackmun, J., dissenting). Moreover, Justice Blackmun found it significant that the federal government and the twenty-three states that exempt the religious use of peyote from their drug laws "all find their (presumably compelling) interests in controlling the use of dangerous drugs compatible with an exemption for religious use of peyote." Id. at 913 n. 5.

Second, with respect to the state's "interest in abolishing drug trafficking," Justice Blackmun pointed out that "there is . . . practically no illegal traffic in peyote." Id. at 916–17.

Finally, turning to the state's "interest in the uniform, fair, and certain enforcement of its drug laws," Justice Blackmun maintained that this argument "could be made in almost any free exercise case. . . . This Court, however, consistently has rejected similar arguments in past free exercise cases, and it should do so here as well." Id. at 916–17.

10. Or. Rev. Stat. § 475.992 (5) (1991).

11. National Prohibition Act of 1919, chap. 85, title 2, § 3, 41 Stat. 305, 308 (1919).

12. McConnell, 103 Harv. L. Rev. at 1419–20.

RELEVANCE OF THE RELIGIOUS FREEDOM RESTORATION ACT

Much of the insecurity for the state of religious freedom that was produced by the constitutional rule of the *Smith* case has recently been ameliorated by the Religious Freedom Restoration Act of 1993,[13] in which Congress legislatively substituted the Supreme Court's pre-*Smith* approach for the new position that the justices had announced in their decision. As a consequence, the federal judiciary has once again been entrusted with substantial guardianship responsibilities for the welfare of religious minorities. Still, a pressing need remains for continued consideration of the analysis supporting the "burdensome effect" principle. First, as an operational matter, the serious doctrinal deficiencies (to be addressed below) that finally led the Court to establish the *Smith* precept have simply been reinstated by the Religious Freedom Restoration Act, albeit as a matter of statutory interpretation rather than constitutional construction. Second, as a theoretical matter, although Congress has ensured temporary protection for religious liberty, the matter is still subject to elimination or substantial modification at any time by a simple exercise of legislative will.

Problems in Fashioning a Better Rule

In declining to overrule the primary precedents undergirding the previous doctrine, Justice Scalia's opinion for the Court in *Smith* left open several avenues that would undoubtedly have been pursued in the future by advocates with no other hope of softening the rule's harshness. As I have argued elsewhere,[14] however, the distinctions drawn by the majority's reasoning are flawed, and it would be multiplying unfortunate judicial misadventures to follow *Smith* with a series of unprincipled and unpredictable exceptions. The burdensome effect principle rejects the *Smith* rule because it would

---

13. 42 U.S.C. § 2000 bb (1993).
14. Choper, 70 Neb. L. Rev. at 674–76, 680–83.

permit government intrusion into too wide a range of areas of religious life. But my approach also seeks to address the genuine problems in constructing a "religion sensitive" precept that were forcefully raised by the Court's opinion in *Smith*.

DISTINCTION FROM RACE

First, Justice Scalia accurately pointed out that despite the fact that the Court subjects "to the most exacting scrutiny laws that make classifications based on race,"[15] it has expressly declined[16] to give any but the most deferential review to "race-neutral laws that have the *effect* of disproportionately disadvantaging a particular racial group."[17] Given the similar treatment that the deliberate disadvantage principle gives to race and religion, it is fair to ask why the Court should give greater scrutiny to "generally applicable, religion-neutral laws that have the effect of burdening a particular religious practice"[18] than it affords to government action that has a disparate impact on minority racial groups.

Although never raised by the Court in support of the doctrinal regime before *Smith*, the answer, it seems to me, lies mainly in the fact that a person's race (or ethnicity) defines an uncomplicated *status*, whereas a person's religion encompasses a *belief system* that is often complex and far-reaching. A core value of the Equal Protection Clause is to forbid people from being prejudiced because of their race. Race-neutral laws that have a disproportionate impact on minority racial/ ethnic groups do not injure members of those groups *because of* their race or ethnicity, but rather because the minority group members are disproportionately represented in the larger group affected (often the poor, or the poorly educated), all of whom are suffering disadvantage.[19] Not all peo-

15. 494 U.S. at 886 n.3.
16. Washington v. Davis, 426 U.S. 229 (1976).
17. 494 U.S. at 886 n. 3 (emphasis in original).
18. Id.
19. There may be exceptional situations in which minority group members suffer unique injury because of their race or ethnicity from the

ple who suffer the special operative consequences of the government action are members of the racial group, and not all members of the racial group suffer the special operative consequences.

A core value of the Religion Clauses is to forbid people from being prejudiced because of their religion. This parallels the prohibition of the Equal Protection Clause as to race. However, since religion involves more than just a status and also imposes an often multifaceted belief system on its adherents, religion-neutral laws that have the effect of burdening a particular religious practice do injure persons *because of* their religion: even though these laws have a fully legitimate public purpose and achieve beneficial results generally, *all* persons who suffer the special operative consequences adverse to their belief system are necessarily members of that religion, and *all* members of the religion suffer the special operative adverse consequences.

There is an additional reason, grounded in weighty practical considerations, for a constitutional rule that is more protective of religion than race against neutral laws that have a disproportionate impact. In holding that an equal protection challenge fails if a law with a racially discriminatory effect has "some rational basis,"[20] the Court was significantly influenced by the recognition that a more restrictive rule would realistically eliminate or severely disrupt many important long-standing and widely supported arrangements: "tests and qualifications for voting, draft deferment, public employment, jury service, and other government-conferred benefits and opportunities . . . ; sales taxes, bail schedules, utility rates, bridge tolls, license fees, and other state-imposed charges."[21] It would hardly be feasible to excuse all members of racial

effect of laws that are race-neutral by their terms and intent. See Frank I. Goodman, De Facto School Segregation: A Constitutional and Empirical Analysis, 60 Calif. L. Rev. 275, 298–307 (1972). Although the matter is plainly beyond the scope of this book, there is a good argument that the Court should apply some version of the burdensome effect principle here too.

20. Washington v. Davis, 426 U.S. at 247.

21. Id. at 248 n. 14 (quoting Goodman, 60 Calif. L. Rev. at 300).

and ethnic minority groups from the obligations of these programs. But granting a religious exemption in response to a successful free exercise challenge in this context ordinarily carries only a modest societal impact and has proved to be a traditionally accepted and workable remedy.

FAR-REACHING POTENTIAL SCOPE

Second, in rejecting the thrust of the burdensome effect principle, Justice Scalia's opinion for the Court in *Smith* argued that judicial application of heightened scrutiny in this context, "across the board, to all actions thought to be religiously commanded,"[22] would lead to alternatively undesirable results: either the degree of scrutiny would end up being diluted[23] or "society . . . would be courting anarchy."[24] Justice Scalia warned that "it is horrible to contemplate that federal judges will regularly balance against the importance of general laws the significance of religious practice," a process that becomes increasingly unwanted "in direct proportion to the society's diversity of religious beliefs, and its determination to coerce or suppress none of them."[25]

The point persuasively illustrates a broader and more complex phenomenon: the close interrelation among a series of factors in this area, including the number of public policies that will be seen as having an adverse impact on religious practices; the number of claims seen as being religious that will receive judicial examination; how grave a burden on religious beliefs will be required to trigger judicial review; how rigorous the standard of review will be; whether other constitutional provisions will duplicate or limit the scope of protection; and what remedies may be granted when a violation is

22. 494 U.S. at 888.

23. In fact this "watering down" of the Court's test of strict judicial scrutiny had already occurred under the doctrinal regime before *Smith*. See Choper, 70 Neb. L. Rev. at 659–70. For a collection of data describing the quite limited protection afforded by federal and state courts under the pre-*Smith* rule, see Mark Tushnet, The Rhetoric of Free Exercise Discourse, 1993 B.Y.U. L. Rev. 117, 121–22.

24. 494 U.S. at 888.

25. 494 U.S. at 889–90 n. 5.

found. Realistically, it is inevitable that an expansive response to any one of these factors must affect how generous the answers to the others will be.

For example, if the courts were unqualifiedly to apply heightened scrutiny to every government regulation that appeared to have the effect of restricting individual religious freedom, the diversity of religious beliefs in the United States—which continues to increase[26]—would make virtually "every regulation of conduct"[27] open to challenge; "religious exemptions from civic obligations of almost every conceivable kind"[28] could be constitutionally ordered. Even the most common and mundane government requirements, such as photographs on drivers' licenses,[29] acquisition of social security numbers,[30] and such activities as building roads[31] or running a selective service system,[32] can conflict with religious beliefs. To make the point most simply and forcefully: government regulations do not intrude on any other personal constitutional right with nearly such breadth.[33] That we may approve of the results reached by courts granting exemptions from government regulations on free exercise grounds[34] does not refute the contention that the judiciary would be more deeply involved here than in other areas.

Similarly, there is an obvious relation between the breadth of the definition given to "religion" and the shaping of substantive doctrine under the Free Exercise Clause. In

26. It has been observed that religious cults—an estimated 1,300 appearing in the United States just between 1965 and 1976—may "encourage their members to disobey or disregard society's laws in favor of the group's mores." Marcia R. Rudin, the Cult Phenomenon: Fad or Fact? 9 N.Y.U. Rev. L. & Soc. Change 17, 18, 31 (1979–80).

27. 494 U.S. at 888.

28. Id.

29. Quaring v. Peterson, 728 F.2d 1121 (8th Cir. 1984), aff'd by equally divided court sub nom. Jensen v. Quaring, 472 U.S. 478 (1985).

30. Bowen v. Roy, 476 U.S. 693 (1986).

31. Lyng v. Northwest Indian Cemetery Protective Association, 485 U.S. 439 (1988).

32. Gillette v. United States, 401 U.S. 437 (1971).

33. See Choper, 70 Neb. L. Rev. at 677–79.

34. See McConnell, 57 U. Chi. L. Rev. at 1142–43.

effect, the definition acts as a screening mechanism that determines which claims will be subjected to whatever substantive "balancing test" will be developed for judging whether an exemption for religion must be granted. Thus the more inclusive the definition of religion, the greater the number and diversity of claims under the Free Exercise Clause that must be considered on the merits.[35] Yet a spacious constitutional definition of religion need not lead to greater protection for religious freedom. The ultimate reach of the Free Exercise Clause can be expanded or limited at either the definitional or substantive steps of the process, and it is unlikely that an extremely broad definition of religion will be permitted to coexist with an extremely generous protection of the claims that fall within that definition. The restrictions the Free Exercise Clause places on government's power to enact neutral, generally applicable regulations governing health, safety, and welfare are marked exceptions to the plenary nature of that authority. Judicial acknowledgment that, at least under our present system of values, civil government requires these exceptions to be fairly narrow is obvious from the Court's observation in one of its leading decisions breathing force into the Free Exercise Clause that "the very concept of ordered liberty precludes allowing every person to make his own standards on matters of conduct in which society as a whole has important interests."[36] Thus recognition of all conceivably religious claims as falling within the burdensome effect principle would call for a relatively modest degree of substantive protection for them, whereas a more confined definition of religion more readily permits a broader protection.

35. Indeed, one function of arguments for a broad definition of religion—e.g., "all that is *arguably religious*" should be considered religious in a free exercise analysis" so that the Free Exercise Clause may "continue to fulfill its 'historic purpose,'" Laurence H. Tribe, American Constitutional Law 828 (1978)—is the creation of an indirect and textually based method of obtaining meaningful and expanding judicial protection for "rights of privacy and personhood," id. at 886, despite the Court's reluctance to do so under the rubric of substantive due process.

36. Wisconsin v. Yoder, 406 U.S. 205, 215–16 (1972).

ELABORATION OF THE PRINCIPLE'S QUALIFICATIONS

Limiting precepts must be found, and the burdensome effect principle incorporates a series of important qualifications.

DEFINITION OF "RELIGION"

Limited Significance

It is crucial to emphasize at the outset that the definition of religion that will be developed here is not to be used for purposes of theology, public policy, or even legal or constitutional problems generally. Rather, it is to be employed only under the burdensome effect principle,[37] whose reach has an important but nonetheless precisely restricted role in securing religious liberty. In a real sense this is much more a substantive interpretation of one aspect of the Free Exercise Clause than it is a formal "definition" of a term in the Constitution. This narrow significance may perhaps be understood most plainly by recognizing that almost all decisions of the Supreme Court that have vindicated individual rights by invoking the Free Exercise Clause could just as easily have been resolved under other provisions of the Constitution and thus require no definition of religion at all.

The Court has made it clear that government action that interferes with an individual's right to hold any set of religious beliefs,[38] or that attempts to "force citizens to confess by word or act their faith therein,"[39] is flatly forbidden. Further, any government imposition of penal or civil sanctions on, or denial of government benefits to, persons for expounding religious views is invalid unless the judiciary concludes that it is justified by a state interest strong enough to

37. Alternative "definitions" to explicate other principles of my thesis will be discussed in chapter 4.

38. Cantwell v. Connecticut, 310 U.S. 296, 303–4 (1940).

39. West Virginia State Board of Education v. Barnette, 319 U.S. 624, 642 (1943).

be characterized as "compelling," "substantial," "important," "overriding," or the like. The decisions documenting these doctrines make manifest, however, that these protections for religious liberty are solidly grounded in the free speech provisions of the First and Fourteenth Amendments and would be readily secured even if there were no Free Exercise Clause in the Constitution. Indeed, many of the Court's most prominent free speech rulings—on such issues as prior restraint,[40] fighting words,[41] public forums,[42] time-place-manner rules,[43] and the permissibility of regulating[44] or taxing[45] the distribution of literature—in fact involve religious expression or such traditional religious activities as proselytizing or soliciting. Similarly, there is no doubt that most rituals, rites, or ceremonies of religious worship—such as fasting, confessing, or performing a mass—that may be denominated as constituting "action" rather than "belief" or "expression" fall squarely within the protection the Court has afforded to nonverbal "symbolic speech."[46]

Moreover, as I have already discussed in some detail, the constitutional guarantee of religious freedom also has consistently been held to contain an antidiscrimination precept that both complements and overlaps the doctrines just described.

40. Kunz v. New York, 340 U.S. 290 (1951); Niemotko v. Maryland, 340 U.S. 268 (1951); Saia v. New York, 334 U.S. 558 (1948); Cantwell v. Connecticut, 310 U.S. 296 (1940); Lovell v. Griffin, 303 U.S. 444 (1938).

41. Chaplinsky v. New Hampshire, 315 U.S. 568 (1942).

42. Widmar v. Vincent, 454 U.S. 263 (1981).

43. Heffron v. International Society for Krishna Consciousness, 452 U.S. 640 (1981).

44. Martin v. Struthers, 319 U.S. 141 (1943); Schneider v. Irvington, 308 U.S. 147 (1939).

45. Follett v. McCormick, 321 U.S. 573 (1944); Murdock v. Pennsylvania, 319 U.S. 105 (1943).

46. Spence v. Washington, 418 U.S. 405 (1974); Schacht v. United States, 398 U.S. 58 (1970); Tinker v. Des Moines School District, 393 U.S. 503 (1969); Stromberg v. California, 283 U.S. 359 (1931).

There is a brief passage in *Smith* with contrary implications, 494 U.S. at 877–78, but it is most unlikely that the Court meant to abandon its long-standing protection of "expressive conduct." Texas v. Johnson, 491 U.S. 397, 403 (1989).

Here again, however, modern constitutional developments under other First Amendment provisions eliminate the necessity of using the Religion Clauses to prevent anything resembling or approaching the persecution of religious dissidents that was so abhorred by the framers. Thus there is no doubt that just as a law denying privileges to persons because they belong to the Communist Party or any other group advocating illegal action would at present be held to violate the freedom of association guarantee of the First and Fourteenth Amendments,[47] so too the Court could invoke this principle to invalidate a statute, such as that upheld many years ago in *Davis v. Beason*,[48] disfranchising any member of an organization that encouraged polygamy. Similarly, freedom of speech doctrine prevents a state from requiring that notaries public declare their belief in the existence of God[49] just as easily as it bars a provision requiring an expression of belief in the virtues of the free enterprise system as a condition of holding public office.[50]

In contrast to the far-reaching guarantees of religious liberty just outlined, the freedom protected by the burdensome effect principle is confined to *action* or *inaction* that is mandated by "religion" and that conflicts with generally applicable government regulations. This liberty, safeguarded under the definition of religion to be propounded here, has been most sparingly defended by the Supreme Court in the past[51] and gets no real refuge at all under its present doctrine. The reality of the Court's stance, which strongly demonstrates the need for limiting factors described above, explains in part why the very liberal substantive scope afforded by the

47. Communist Party v. Whitcomb, 414 U.S. 441 (1974); United States v. Robel, 389 U.S. 258 (1967); Aptheker v. Secretary of State, 378 U.S. 500 (1964).

48. 133 U.S. 333 (1890).

49. See Torcaso v. Watkins, 367 U.S. 488 (1961).

50. See Bond v. Floyd, 385 U.S. 116 (1966). For use of the Equal Protection Clause as another tool to achieve these results, see chapter 2, note 12 above.

51. See note 23 above and note 139 below.

burdensome effect principle calls for a definition of religion that is relatively compressed.

Alternative Formulations

The Seeger-Welsh *Approach.* Probably reflecting the less complicated conception of "religion" that prevailed in the earlier years of the republic—a concordance fractured by the evolution of our present multireligious society[52]—the Supreme Court's first real attempt at a definition of religion, at the end of the nineteenth century in *Davis v. Beason,*[53] was that "the term 'religion' has reference to one's views of his relations to his Creator, and to the obligations they impose of reverence for his being and character, and of obedience to his will."[54] Since then, its most thoroughly considered effort has been in a statutory, rather than a constitutional, setting. In *United States v. Seeger,*[55] the Court interpreted a provision of the Universal Military Training and Service Act[56] that exempted from the armed forces "those persons who by reason of their religious training and belief are conscientiously opposed to participation in war in any form."[57] "Religious training and belief" was defined by the statute as "an individual's belief in a relation to a Supreme Being involving duties superior to those arising from any human relation, but does not include essentially political, sociological or philosophical views or a merely personal moral code."[58] The Court's test for determining the meaning of the statutory definition was "whether a given belief . . . occupies a place in the life of its possessor parallel to that filled by the orthodox belief in

52. It has been estimated that more than eight hundred organized religions have appeared in North America during this century, J. Gordon Melton, Another Look at New Religions, 527 Annals Am. Acad. Pol. & Sol. Sci. 97 (May 1993).

53. 133 U.S. 333 (1890).

54. Id. at 342.

55. 380 U.S. 163 (1965).

56. 50 U.S.C. App. §456(j) (1958).

57. Id.

58. Id.

God."[59] This guideline for "whether a conscientious objector's beliefs are religious"[60] was given further content (and elasticity) in *Welsh v. United States,* in which the opinion announcing the Court's judgment pointed out "that 'intensely personal' convictions which some might find 'incomprehensible' or 'incorrect' come within the meaning of 'religious belief' " if they are "held with the strength of traditional religious convictions."[61] Although the *Seeger* Court expressed the view that this "parallel position" test would be "simple of application,"[62] a probe beneath its veneer—especially as more fully articulated in *Welsh*—discloses substantially greater difficulties than the Court's confident language suggests.

One major ambiguity of the *Seeger-Welsh* approach concerns precisely what "place" God or religion occupies in the life of a member of a conventional religious sect. In fact, religion does not play a single, ascertainable role in the existence of traditional believers; rather, it may affect their being in a variety of ways—for example, morally, spiritually, or socially. Nor need its influence remain constant; its impact may change over time. Moreover, even within a given sect, religion will fill different functions in the lives of different members.

More important, there appears to be no readily observable line of demarcation between those beliefs that are "parallel" to a belief in God or other orthodox religious precepts and those that are not. It is true that some analogies can be drawn between the religions of, for example, Orthodox Jews, Jehovah's Witnesses, and Roman Catholics. All three involve a belief in God, but that is precisely the similarity that *Seeger* rejected as too narrow. All three also involve membership in a group that propounds certain moral principles, but this is equally true for the Boy Scouts and the American Medical Association, neither of which is either commonly perceived

59. 380 U.S. at 166.
60. Welsh v. United States, 398 U.S. 333, 339 (1970).
61. Id. at 339–40.
62. 380 U.S. at 184.

as a religion or thought to be entitled to any special privileges under the Free Exercise Clause.

There are two distinct paths that may be pursued in adding texture to the *Seeger-Welsh* "parallel position" formulation's uncertain scope. One is a functional approach that seeks similarity in the intensity of conviction with which beliefs are held. Another is a content-based approach that searches for analogues in subject matter that are both common and exclusive to concededly religious beliefs.[63] In considering these broad alternatives (and their more specific applications) for defining religion for the purpose of the burdensome effect principle's constitutional immunity from general government regulations of conduct, it is important to attempt to identify various historical and contemporary values underlying the Free Exercise Clause that justify this very special protection. The choices can then be evaluated in light of those values as well as more general criteria for the needed definition.

"Ultimate Concerns": A Functional Criterion. As a comparison between the Court's efforts in *Davis v. Beason* and *Seeger* reveals, judicial efforts to define religion in the context at hand have attempted to keep pace with modern theological ideas. Developing concepts of religion within the Christian tradition have tended to move beyond orthodox concepts of God. Some contemporary theologians, with a significant Christian following, urge secularization as the proper path of the church and social change as the just topic of study for theology.[64] Others, while reaffirming the importance of transcendental faith, have departed from an anthropomorphic concept of a deity. Thus John A. T. Robinson, the bishop of Woolwich, in his controversial book *Honest to God,*[65] which

63. See John H. Mansfield, Conscientious Objection—1964 Term, in 1965 Relig. & Pub. Ord. 3, 9; Kent Greenawalt, Religion as a Concept in Constitutional Law, 72 Calif. L. Rev. 753 (1984).

64. See, e.g., Harvey G. Cox, The Secular City (1965).

65. John A. T. Robinson, Honest to God (1963).

was quoted by the Court in *Seeger*,[66] rejects the idea of "a God 'out there,' a God who 'exists' above and beyond the world he made, a God 'to' whom we pray and to whom we 'go' when we die."[67] Paul Tillich, also invoked by the *Seeger* Court in support of its holding,[68] identifies faith as "the state of being ultimately concerned,"[69] and God as "the ground of all being."[70]

Because of the favorable attention given by the Court to these progressive theologians, several interpretations of religion for constitutional purposes have been advocated that are based on Tillich's idea of "ultimate concerns."[71] These proposals look primarily to the functional aspects of religion—its importance in the believer's scheme of things— rather than to its content. Ultimate concerns are to be protected, no matter how "secular" their subject matter may appear to be.[72]

This approach has several attractive features. First, it fulfills the need for a tolerant definition by its capacity to include nonconformist and unusual groups as well as known orthodox sects, and by its rejection of judicial determinations of whether some beliefs are inherently more "valuable" than others. Even more important, respect for deeply held beliefs is plainly a central value underlying the Religion Clauses. By focusing on the great significance the belief holds for the claimant, this approach responds to the aversion, discussed more fully below, to confronting an individual with the especially oppressive choice of either forsaking such precepts or suffering the pains of government sanctions.

The virtues of this definition, however, are outweighed by a series of difficulties. First, although Tillich's ideas may

66. 380 U.S. at 181.

67. Robinson, Honest to God at 14.

68. 380 U.S. at 180, 187.

69. Paul Tillich, Dynamics of Faith 1 (1957).

70. Paul Tillich, The Shaking of the Foundations 63 (1963).

71. See J. Morris Clark, Guidelines for the Free Exercise Clause, 83 Harv. L. Rev. 327, 340–44 (1969); Note, Toward a Constitutional Definition of Religion, 91 Harv. L. Rev. 1056, 1072–83 (1978).

72. Note, 91 Harv. L. Rev. at 1075–76.

well be the profound expressions of a radical theologian searching for truth, even today they only partially comprehend "religion" as that term is understood by most theologians and the laity. For example, this approach would exclude any practices of worship that "do not derive directly from ultimate concern" and would slight any beliefs that may be largely "detached from the development of ultimate concerns."[73] Moreover, "though most modern religions both give answers to major questions of existence and offer an overarching focus for people's lives, some belief systems, commonly regarded as religious, have existed that do not make such claims. In these systems, how life should be lived has been determined on some other basis; and religious worship has been mainly a matter of placating the gods or enlisting their help for projects with preestablished value."[74]

Second, Tillich's writings occupy volumes and are directed at theologians and lay believers, not lawyers. To extract from them the phrase "ultimate concerns" and instruct judges to apply it as a legal formula seriously underestimates the subtlety of Tillich's thought and overestimates the theological sophistication of the participants in the legal process. For example, although Tillich recognizes that individuals may have such things as nationalism or worldly success as their ultimate concerns,[75] he accords such concerns no special respect, finding them to be idolatrous because they claim to be ultimate without really being so.[76]

Most important, in terms of the need to fashion a definition of religion that places limits on the reach of the burdensome effect principle, our experience reveals that ultimate concerns may relate to such matters as science, politics, economics, social welfare, or even recreation—all staples of nor-

73. Greenawalt, 72 Calif. L. Rev. at 765.
74. Id. at 809.
75. Tillich, Dynamics of Faith at 1–4.
76. Id. at 11–12. Moreover, not all religious belief is "ultimate" in the functional sense, although it may deal with "ultimate" subject matter. See Welsh, 398 U.S. at 358–59 (Harlan, J., concurring); Mansfield, 1965 Relig. & Pub. Ord. at 9 n. 96.

mal government regulation.[77] For this reason, the "ultimate concerns" approach is at odds with an important historical assumption that underlies the constitutional protection granted by the Religion Clauses: that religion comprehends matters with which the government, whose authority is presumptively plenary, is not competent to interfere.[78] Pursuant to this postulate, religion was to be regarded as a separate realm to which the First Amendment ceded a degree of sovereignty. Because "ultimate concerns" pervade virtually all areas of ordinary government involvement, however, to grant them the special constitutional immunity of the burdensome effect principle merely because they are strongly held—whatever the true importance of such beliefs to the individual or society as a whole—would severely undermine the state's ability to advance the commonweal.[79]

77. The tenets of various political movements have often been directed toward ultimate concerns, e.g., communism: see John C. Bennett, Christianity and Communism 87–88 (1970), and John M. Murry, The Necessity of Communism (1932); Marxism: see Leslie Dewart, The Future of Belief 56–58 (1966), and Joseph A. Schumpeter, Capitalism, Socialism and Democracy 5–8 (5th ed. 1976); Nazism, Italian Fascism and Japanese militarism: see Edward Shillito, Nationalism: Man's Other Religion (1933). See also Robert N. Bellah, Civil Religion in America, 96 Daedalus 1 (winter 1967). Moreover, some users of drugs such as LSD have used them to seek a state of ultimate concern. William Braden, The Private Sea: LSD and the Search for God 9–10, 89–92 (1967).

78. As Madison wrote in his Memorial and Remonstrance against Religious Establishments: "That the Civil Magistrate is a competent Judge of Religious truth . . . is an arrogant pretension falsified by the contradicting opinions of Rulers in all ages, and throughout the world." ¶ 5, set forth in Everson, 330 U.S. at 67 (app.).

79. Closely related to the "ultimate concerns" approach is the suggestion that "religion" should be construed to embrace "a comprehensive belief system. . .[that] proffer[s] a systematic series of answers. . .to the questions and doubts that haunt modern man." Malnak v. Yogi, 592 F.2d 197, 209, 214 (3d Cir. 1979) (Adams, J., concurring). See also Africa v. Pennsylvania, 662 F.2d 1025, 1035 (3d Cir. 1981) (Adams, J.). An important decision by another prominent judge emphasizes the fact that a group seeking classification as a religion must subscribe to "the underlying theories of man's nature or his place in the Universe which characterize recognized religions." Founding Church of Scientology v. United States, 409 F.2d 1146, 1160 (D.C. Cir. 1969) (Wright, J.).

Similarly, John Mansfield has suggested that "religious" beliefs are distinguished by "the fundamental character of the truths asserted, and the

Finally, because of its inherent vagueness, the ultimate concerns standard suffers from being based in large measure on psychological factors that are very difficult to administer. The legal process would be confronted with such formidable issues as what an "ultimate concern" really is and how "ultimate" a concern must be in order to qualify as religious. "Does everyone have an ultimate concern? Does anyone have more than one? Is a person's ultimate concern determined by his cognitive beliefs or his psychological attitudes? How does ultimate concern relate to absolute moral prohibitions? To one's deepest desires? For a claim to qualify as based on ultimate concern, what must be the connection between the

---

fact that they address themselves to basic questions about the nature of reality and the meaning of human existence." Mansfield, 1965 Relig. & Pub. Ord. at 10. This position has the theological support of John Haynes Holmes, who defined religion as "the consciousness of some power manifest in nature which helps man in the ordering of his life in harmony with its demands . . . [; it] is the supreme expression of human nature; it is man thinking his highest, feeling his deepest, and living his best." Quoted in United States v. Seeger, 380 U.S. 163, 169 (1965).

The difficulty, however, is that at least some traditional religious beliefs do not appear necessarily to be comprehensive and, more seriously, that many comprehensive beliefs are not necessarily religious. Clark, 83 Harv. L. Rev. at 339. For example, atheistic Marxism may be fairly described as comprehensive because it supplies answers to profound questions and denies the significance of other issues. Indeed, it has been urged that Marxism is, at least to some, a religion. See A. Stephen Boyan, Defining Religion in Operational and Institutional Terms, 116 U. Pa. L. Rev. 479 (1968). See also Louis Dupre, Spiritual Life in a Secular Age, 111 Daedalus 21, 22 (winter 1982). However, because its tenets involve economic and social theories squarely within the realm of everyday government concern, Marxism is generally regarded as a political, not a religious, ideology.

The same problems of under- and overinclusiveness arise in respect to another basically functional approach. Several courts have attempted to define religion (for both constitutional and statutory purposes) by looking to "formal, external, or surface signs that may be analogized to accepted religions." Malnak, 592 F.2d at 209. Such indicators, usually regarded as useful rather than essential, "might include formal services, ceremonial functions, the existence of clergy, structure and organization, efforts at propagation, observation of holidays, and other similar manifestations associated with traditional religion." Id. at 209. See also Founding Church of Scientology, 409 F.2d at 1160; Washington Ethical Society v. District of Columbia, 249 F.2d 127 (D.C. Cir. 1957); Fellowship of Humanity v. County of Alameda, 153 Cal. App.2d 673, 315 P.2d 394 (1957).

act involved and that which constitutes the ultimate concern?"[80] The broad discretion afforded the fact finder, whether judge or jury, poses a significant risk that parochial preconceptions will often prevail to the detriment of claimants with unorthodox principles, and that appellate review will be able to correct only the most blatantly arbitrary decisions. Moreover, because the claimants' own characterization of their beliefs will frequently be the sole evidence supporting their position, and because success will often depend on their ability to articulate the relation between deeply held beliefs and a definition whose meaning is only dimly understood, the likely beneficiaries will be both the orthodox believers and those others who are best educated and most articulate.

"Extratemporal Consequences": A More Content-Based Criterion. As I indicated above, a forceful explanation and pragmatic justification for the Free Exercise Clause's special exemption from otherwise universal government regulation is that the commands of religious belief, at least as conventionally perceived, have a unique significance for believers. This makes it particularly cruel for the government to require them to choose between violating those dictates and suffering meaningful tangible disabilities.[81] Moreover, although the state may, and sometimes must, make many harsh demands on its citizens—such as serving in the military, paying taxes, and forbearing from specified forms of pleasurable behavior—our traditions, informed by both moral and instrumental concerns, have set various constitutional, statutory, and common-law limits on the reach of government power.

The relation between religion and these conventions may be illustrated by hypothesizing two objectors to military ser-

80. Greenawalt, 72 Calif. L. Rev. at 807.
81. This policy is reflected in numerous Free Exercise Clause opinions. See, e.g., Gillette, 400 U.S. at 445 ("hard choice between contravening imperatives of religion and conscience or suffering penalties"); id. at 454 ("painful dilemma"); Braunfeld v. Brown, 366 U.S. 599, 616 (1961) (Stewart, J., dissenting) ("to choose between his religious faith and his economic survival . . . is a cruel choice").

vice. One has sincere conscientious scruples against killing, but no one, including the draftee, claims they are religious.[82] The other's objection is rooted in a deep-seated belief that if he voluntarily kills another human being, this will influence or indeed determine his destiny after death. At the extreme, he may believe that his immortal soul will be damned for eternity. Clearly, both young men will experience severe psychic turmoil if required to kill. But though there is no sure method of proving it empirically, intuition and experience affirm that the degree of internal trauma on earth for those who have put their souls in jeopardy for eternity (or, for example, have caused loved ones to be damned forever) can be expected to be markedly greater for most of these persons than for those who have only violated a conscientious/moral scruple. This is not to dismiss the likelihood that there will be some objectors with no claim to being religious who will nonetheless experience even greater emotional anguish than those whose beliefs predict everlasting consequences. These comparative feelings of pain will turn on such factors as the intensity and centrality of the beliefs and the psychological sensitivity of the individual.[83] Still, the categorical distinction based on instinct and understanding that I have suggested allows the courts to avoid subtle, case-by-case inquiries into the gradations of psychic turmoil suffered by different people, even at the price of an erroneous conclusion in a given instance.[84]

82. This person, for example, might base his reaction on principles inspired by his parents and confirmed by his experience.

83. See Note, Religion and Morality Legislation: A Reexamination of Establishment Clause Analysis, 59 N.Y.U. L. Rev. 301, 346–52 (1984).

84. Stanley Ingber, Religion or Ideology: A Needed Clarification of the Religion Clauses, 41 Stan. L. Rev. 233, 275 n. 265 (1989). There is, of course, a third type of conscientious objector, one who deeply believes that taking another's life is a fundamental violation of "God's law" but causes no afterlife effects, perhaps because all sins are naturally forgiven under this person's belief system. Although this individual surely would be commonly considered a "religious" objector, for purposes of the particular discussion here he would be classified with the nonreligious objector. This person should be contrasted with one for whom absolution is just a *possibility*, e.g., an individual whose tenets involve "a life-long balance sheet in which every act has an extratemporal consequence which may be offset by a sufficient number of acts meriting the opposite consequence." Note, 59 N.Y.U. L.

It must be acknowledged, however, that the state is not exclusively responsible for the concededly grave consequences facing the religious objector to military service. The government has simply presented both draftees with the option of either fulfilling their legal obligation or paying the price of fines, imprisonment, or a loss of government benefits. Because these state-imposed consequences are the same for both objectors, it may be said that there is no special cruelty in punishing the latter. Moreover, at a psychological level, the identical cost may be more comfortably borne by those religionists who can balance it against eternal (or everlasting) rewards rather than merely temporal (or transitory) benefits. Indeed, some may believe that martyrdom has independent value in affecting their destiny. Nonetheless, because the perceived burden of *obeying* the law is so severe for the religious objector, our traditions hold that his noncompliance is not so morally culpable as that of one who disobeys for other reasons. This principle is reflected in the defenses of duress and justification in the criminal law,[85] excusing or warranting violations when society regards the cost of compliance as being higher than an individual should reasonably be expected to bear. The philosophy is also contained in the view that "the frustration of religious obligations inflict[s] a peculiar harm on believers":[86] since government has no power to protect these persons from the adverse effects of their obedience to law, then it may not insist on their submission.[87]

This "special cruelty" factor—seeking to draw a line beyond which it is unreasonable for government to expect per-

---

Rev. at 347 n. 199. The spiritual distress endured by these people should be considerably mitigated by the opportunity for offsetting conduct. Still, beliefs of this sort would fall within the prescribed definition because, in my view, they come adequately close to producing the unique psychic pain that should qualify under the burdensome effect principle.

85. See Model Penal Code and Commentaries §§ 2.09, 3.02 (1985).

86. Timothy L. Hall, Religion, Equality, and Difference, 65 Temple L. Rev. 1,34 (1992).

87. See Lon Fuller, The Case of the Speluncean Explorers, 65 Harv. L. Rev. 616, 625 (1949).

sons to alter or violate their beliefs—is difficult to measure precisely, because the degrees of importance of various individuals' beliefs obviously form a continuous spectrum. Nonetheless, as the discussion above suggests, I maintain that a sincerely held belief in "extratemporal consequences"—that the results of actions taken pursuant or contrary to the dictates of persons' faith may well extend in some meaningful way beyond their lifetimes, either by affecting their own eternal existence or by producing a permanent and everlasting significance and place in reality for all persons that follow[88]—is a sensible and desirable criterion (albeit plainly far short of ideal, as we shall see in the section that follows) for determining when the Free Exercise Clause should trigger special judicial consideration of whether an exemption from general government regulations of conduct is constitutionally required.

This "extratemporal consequences" criterion, which does not focus only on the intensity of conviction with which the beliefs are held but rather considers the perceived repercussions of their violation, is somewhat more content based than functional in its emphasis. By tending toward the subject matter of beliefs in this way, it probably conforms more than the "ultimate concerns" standard with the conventional, average person's conception of religion, which, though largely intuitive, would generally conclude, for example, that a belief in God is religious but a belief in the Republican Party is not, no matter how strongly held either may be.

Although this approach may thus have the virtue of some greater common acceptability, the primary disadvantage of adopting a content-based definition of religion for the burdensome effect principle is the danger of parochialism and intolerance—that judges will include conventional constructs in the definition and exclude new, unfamiliar, or "dangerous" beliefs. This is in fact the course the Supreme Court took in

88. See Charles Hartshorne, The Logic of Perfection and Other Essays in Neoclassical Metaphysics chap. 10 (1962); Alfred N. Whitehead, Process and Reality: An Essay in Cosmology pt. 5 (1929).

the polygamy cases.[89] Thus it has been argued that "at the very point where [content-based efforts to define religion] say, in effect, that a person must hold certain tenets or focus on certain issues in order to come within the constitutional protection, they demonstrate their incapacity to effectuate that protection. They enshrine an orthodoxy within a Constitution designed in part to protect unorthodoxy."[90]

Several considerations, however, support the extratemporal consequences precept against this criticism. First, unlike content-based approaches that center on the specific substance of beliefs—such as a commitment to God—it looks only to the supposed ultimate effects of beliefs, whatever their particular substance may be. In this sense at least, it is sufficiently flexible and capable of growth to include newly perceived and unconventional values.

Second, even to the extent that this criterion "enshrines" beliefs of a particular genre, it must be recalled that the dominant purpose of the Religion Clauses is to single out "religion," as opposed to other systems of belief. This concept must therefore have some minimum content. It also bears repeating that beliefs falling outside this definition (such as those associated with the Universalist, Secular Humanism, Deism,[91] and Ethical Culture movements, as well as other more "conventional" religions to be discussed shortly) are not remitted to the standard regime of regulation and punishment. Rather, all individual concerns, opinions, and beliefs receive substantial protection under other constitutional provisions. As a matter of history and necessity, however, the special immunity for conduct afforded by the burdensome effect principle may belong only to a special category of beliefs.

89. In Davis v. Beason, the Court concluded that "bigamy and polygamy are crimes by the laws of all civilized and Christian countries. . . .To extend exemption from punishment for such crimes would be to shock the moral judgment of the community. To call their advocacy a tenet of religion is to offend the common sense of mankind." 133 U.S. at 341.

90. Note, 91 Harv. L. Rev. at 1074–75.

91. Some "Deists" did believe in an afterlife and a system of rewards and punishments. See Henry F. May, The Enlightenment in America 295 (1976); Herbert of Cherbury, De Veritate (1633).

Third, although the content of even the most well-recognized religious belief systems is so varied as to defy any efforts to distill uniform tenets, the extratemporal consequences precept finds support not only in those traditional religions prevalent in our culture but in most of the world's other major sects as well. At present most branches of Christianity, Islam, and Judaism posit some form of divine judgment after death.[92] Although the everlasting effects dynamic may lean toward Western religions, various sects of Hinduism and Buddhism teach that each person is to be reincarnated, with the merit accumulated by virtuous acts in this life affecting one's status in the next, and with the possibility of eventual entry into heaven or nirvana for Buddhists.[93]

Finally, the extratemporal consequences concept has roots reaching to such key founders as William Penn,[94] James Madison, and Thomas Jefferson[95] and has appeared in major Supreme Court decisions. In *Wisconsin v. Yoder*, for example, in which the Court held that the Free Exercise Clause demanded an exemption for Amish children from the state's requirement of school attendance until age sixteen, the opinion noted that the Old Order Amish "believed that by sending their children to high school, they would . . . endanger their own salvation and that of their children."[96] Similarly, Justices Black and Douglas observed in the *Flag Salute Case* that "compelling little children [who are Jehovah's Witnesses] to partici-

92. John B. Noss, Man's Religions 557–58, 561, 574, 622 (1963); Hans J. Schoeps, The Religions of Mankind 209, 234–35 (1966); Larry D. Shinn, Abingdon Dictionary of Living Religions 238–39 (1981); 5 Hastings Encyclopedia of Religion and Ethics 380–86 (1951); 2 Historia Religionum 41, 43 (Claas J. Bleeker ed. 1971).

93. Noss, Man's Religions at 123, 145–47, 181–83, 189–90, 206–9.

94. See William Penn, The Great Case of Liberty of Conscience, in 2 William Penn on Religion and Ethics 426 (Hugh S. Barbour ed. 1991): "Must [religious believers] be Persecuted here if they do not go against their Conscience, and punished hereafter if they do?"

95. See discussion and citation of authorities in David C. Williams & Susan H. Williams, Volitionalism and Religious Liberty, 76 Corn. L. Rev. 769, 853–58 (1991).

96. 406 U.S. 205, 209.

pate in a ceremony . . . ends in nothing for them but a fear of spiritual condemnation."[97]

"Transcendent Reality": A Possible Criterion. Despite the advantages of the extratemporal consequences test for determining when a belief qualifies for the special constitutional protection of the burdensome effect principle, it must be forthrightly admitted that this criterion is not congruent with much that theologians and the laity would include in a definition of religion. Even within the Christian tradition there are many articles of faith that do not relate directly to any reward or punishment after death. Belief in the possibility of divine intervention on earth is one example: faith healing, retribution, and answered prayers. Another is the precept, found in the teachings of Saint Augustine and John Calvin, that salvation is the gift of God to his chosen and is not to be earned by good works during life.[98] Adhering to such beliefs, one could act from a religious compulsion that was not at all connected to the achievement of redemption. The use of wine for communion also illustrates a widely followed religious practice that would probably not be shielded by the burdensome effect principle[99] (and also would not qualify as a ritual of worship that could secure judicial protection as nonverbal "symbolic speech").[100]

Other religions, moreover, may altogether ignore the afterlife consequences of one's acts. Many major faiths at various stages have been far more concerned with the relationship between the living and the world around them than with

---

97. Barnette, 319 U.S. at 644 (Black, J., concurring).

98. Noss, Man's Religions at 646, 676–77; Schoeps, The Religions of Mankind at 274; Shinn, Abingdon Dictionary at 580.

99. Greenawalt, 72 Calif. L. Rev. at 809.

100. The likely reasoning would be that the government's interest in prohibiting the consumption of alcoholic beverages is not "related to the suppression of free expression," Texas v. Johnson, 491 U.S. 397, 403 (1989), but simply imposes an "incidental limitation on First Amendment freedoms." United States v. O'Brien, 391 U.S. 367, 376 (1968).

the fate of the dead.[101] Religions that do concern themselves with the deceased often aim to propitiate the spirits of the departed or prevent them from returning,[102] an attitude toward the dead that is still widespread. The indigenous religion of China, for example, is a well-developed system of ancestor worship in which the spirits of dead forebears are regarded as taking an active and continuing role in the well-being of the family.[103] Chinese religion involves strong duties but does not usually connect them with consequences to follow after death.[104] Thus, although there is extensive belief in the idea that this life is but one phase of existence, with the next phase to be determined by a person's actions on earth, this tenet is not universal among the world's major religions, nor is it the only important doctrine of those sects that do hold it.

Admittedly, many beliefs that are generally regarded as religious despite their exclusive bearing on temporal affairs do share a common core with the extratemporal consequences canon. These precepts are concerned with aspects of reality that are not observable in ordinary experience but are assumed to exist at another level. By addressing "basic questions,"[105] or by engaging in a quest for "a truth so profound and so personal that it defies expression in ordinary language,"[106] or perhaps by offering mystical revelation of the unity of the world, such beliefs tend to infuse reality with transcendent meaning and significance—often through doctrines that explain such phenomena as the creation of the

101. Noss, Man's Religions at 14–31; 5 Hastings Encyclopedia at 380–83.

102. Noss at 28–30.

103. Id. at 336–41.

104. A Chinese person who betrayed his ancestors, however, might have been considered an outcast by his family, a result that would pursue him after death. Noss, Man's Religions at 340–44. Further, it is said that the "more pious" Chinese can lessen punishment after death by devout acts. Shinn, Abingdon Dictionary at 167.

105. Mansfield, 1965 Relig. & Pub. Ord. at 10.

106. Philip Selznick, The Moral Commonwealth 426 n. 77 (1992).

world or the nature of life and death. These aspects of reality may be felt by the believer, but because they cannot be demonstrated as facts, they transcend material experience, often calling for "a leap of faith."[107] This is confirmed by theological conceptions such as John Robinson's, which substitutes the metaphor of depth for the metaphor of height and views God as "the ultimate depth of all our being, the creative ground and meaning of our existence."[108] Robinson rejects the naturalistic contentions that "God is merely a redundant name for nature or for humanity"[109] and thus affirms the transcendent nature of religion.[110] Similarly, Paul Tillich has written that "the source of this affirmation of meaning within meaninglessness, or certitude within doubt, is not the God of traditional theism but the 'God above God,' the power of being, which works through those who have no name for it, even the name of God."[111]

It may be persuasively argued that *all* beliefs that invoke a transcendent reality—and especially those that provide their adherents with glimpses of meaning and truth that make them so important and so unshakable—be encompassed by the special constitutional protection granted "religion" by the burdensome effect principle. Such beliefs not only conform to broadly based theological and lay perceptions of religion. They also appear to be distinguishable from more secularly grounded ideologies (such as humanistic pacifism, socialism, or Marxism) that, although perhaps equally comprehensive and as deeply held, we think of as being concerned largely with observable facts or ordinary human experience.

Systems of thought that are grounded exclusively in observable facts—and about which evidence can be gathered, experts consulted, rational discourse undertaken, empirical

107. Id. at 426.

108. Robinson, Honest to God at 47.

109. Id. at 54.

110. See also Tillich's discussion of true and idolatrous faiths, Dynamics of Faith at 11–12.

111. Paul Tillich, 2 Systematic Theology 12 (1957), quoted in Seeger, 380 U.S. at 180.

conclusions drawn, and policies made (and altered in light of new knowledge)—fall squarely within the realm of traditional government decision making. Although individuals may hold strong views on these matters, our political structures presume that there is a "correct" answer that civil authority may decree. Yet facts that are neither conventionally observable nor empirically verifiable, but are rather unknowable in the physical world, can only be experienced by the believer or taken on faith. No one, including government, can dictate or deny such experiences. Nor do their underpinnings change over time in light of newly developed facts or theories. Thus it may be said that beliefs concerned with transcendent reality are outside the regulatory competence of the state.

In many ways, however, transcendental explanations of worldly realities are essentially no different, even in terms of government regulatory competence, from conventional exegeses for temporal outcomes that are based on such "rational" disciplines as economics, political science, sociology, or psychology, or even on such "hard" sciences as biophysics, geophysics, or just plain physics. When we justify competing government policies on such varied matters as social welfare, the economy, and military and foreign affairs, there is at base only a gossamer line between "natural" (or worldly) and "supernatural" (or divine) causation—the former really being little more capable of "scientific proof" than the latter. In fact, "it is not at all clear that religion is the only belief system that bases its understanding of the world upon a cognition other than that achieved through practical reasoning. Most other types of beliefs and moral values have non-rational components. Indeed, the contentions that practical reasoning leads to an understanding of reality and that morality may be understood through rational processes are themselves ultimately based on no more than their own non-rational, *a priori* assumptions."[112] Moreover, at the level of final decision, even

---

112. William P. Marshall, The Case against the Constitutionally Compelled Free Exercise Exemption, 7 J.L. & Relig. 363, 388 (1989) (citing Albert Camus, The Myth of Sisyphus and Other Essays 119 (Justin O'Brien trans. 1969) (attacking the purported certainty of rationality and examining

the most frankly utilitarian goals depend ultimately on values—such as good or evil, or even the desirability of human survival—that represent normative preferences rather than logically compelled choices.[113] "Secular ideology . . . may embrace a logic that is highly resistant to examination and correction."[114] The "rival premises are such that we possess no rational way of weighing the claims of one as against the other."[115] Indeed, "it may be persuasively argued that the validity of all claims to scientific truth depends on a leap of faith in accepting the validity of inductive reasoning."[116] Therefore, if government generally possesses plenary authority to regulate the worldly affairs of society—and it surely does under our historical and contemporary political scheme—then its ability to do so should not be restricted because of the nature of the causes, which are all basically unverifiable, that different groups believe will produce consequences that the state seeks to achieve. In addition, from the standpoint of the vital need for principled adjudicative standards for constitutional decision making by a nonmajoritarian judiciary, there are several other central factors regarding which it appears very difficult, if not impossible, to distinguish transcendental ideologies from those commonly considered to

---

human existence in a world whose understanding is beyond human reasoning).

113. "Thus, for example, the Judeo-Christian notion that human beings are created in God's image, and that their lives are thereby rendered precious, may reasonably be viewed as in some sense parallel to the secular notion of human dignity that underlies American constitutional law, its human rights guarantees, and the American commitment to popular sovereignty. Although the religious and secular formulations of such notions may characteristically ring in different terminology, having different connotations or colorations, they nevertheless have as their respective referents some of the same essential ideas." Note, Good Faith? Religious-Secular Parallelism and the Establishment Clause, 93 Colum. L. Rev. 1763, 1788 (1993).

114. Selznick, The Moral Commonwealth at 427.

115. Alasdair MacIntyre, After Virtue 8 (1981). See generally Kent Greenawalt, Religious Convictions and Political Choice 145–52 (1988).

116. Note, Defining "Religion" in the First Amendment: A Functional Approach, 74 Corn. L. Rev. 532, 542 (1989) (citing David Hume, An Enquiry concerning Human Understanding 25–39 (L. A. Silby-Bigge ed. 1893)).

be based on secular premises: the intensity with which the beliefs are held, the mental anguish resulting from their violation, and the comprehensive scope of the creeds' dogmas.

An Imperfect Solution

Any "single feature definition"[117] appears beset with serious shortcomings: we have already seen that "ultimate concerns" and "transcendental reality" suffer from ambiguity and are also both underinclusive and overinclusive. The extratemporal consequences criterion, although it possesses the virtue of relative clarity, with the consequent restraint against parochial judicial application, is still surely not free of defects, as has been conceded at length. It may be that an "analogical approach" is preferable, one that first "identifies what is indubitably religious largely by reference to [its] beliefs, practices, and organizations"[118] (recognizing that "no single feature is indispensable")[119] and then defines religion "by the closeness of analogy in the relevant respects between the disputed instance and what is indisputably religion."[120] This would encompass tenets and practices ordinarily thought to be religious that would otherwise be excluded under other definitions. But the uncertainties of this approach and its capacity for a relatively boundless judicial discretion that threatens the dispassionate treatment of beliefs secured by the Religion Clauses are highlighted by the substantive standards that its author propounds for varied contexts; he suggests, for example, that a "court should ask whether strong reasons support limitation of the exemption"[121] for religion, or "whether a constitutionally grounded exception to a prohibition would be tolerable."[122]

To end this section as it began, there is an irresistible need for limiting precepts in respect to the burdensome effect

117. Greenawalt, 72 Calif. L. Rev. at 766.
118. Id. at 767.
119. Id. at 768.
120. Id. at 762; see also John B. Cobb Jr., God and the World (1969).
121. Greenawalt, 72 Calif. L. Rev. at 800.
122. Id. at 784.

principle; the absence of such constraints on judicial power was a primary reason, if not *the only* cause, for the Court's rejection of its earlier, more protective Free Exercise Clause doctrine. Any of the alternative definitional approaches discussed may be fit into the burdensome effect principle. The extratemporal consequences definition, although rooted in the core values of the Free Exercise Clause, is admittedly so confined as to be significantly underinclusive and may even be credibly subject to the charge of "serious distortion of the complex values of the religion clauses."[123] Still, it is worth repeating that the extratemporal consequences description, like the analogical approach, is reserved for a "particular legal context":[124] it applies only to one aspect of free exercise and not to all problems under the Religion Clauses. Moreover, from a utilitarian perspective the intuitive judgment persists that obeying the law at the price of perceived eternal repercussions produces substantially greater psychological suffering than does doing so at the cost of compromising scruples with only temporal reactions. Thus, in my view, the extreme protection from government power to regulate conduct afforded by the burdensome effect principle should be reserved for those who personally believe, regardless of any formal religious affiliation, that departure from certain articles of faith will carry uniquely severe consequences extending beyond their present existence.

COGNIZABLE INJURY

The requisite of some form of threshold injury, even if only modest or minimal, for federal judicial vindication of constitutional rights has strong credentials in both law and policy.[125] As previously discussed, there are strong objections to my approach's requirement that an injury be greater and more palpable than feelings of offense and alienation in order to invalidate government action that either seeks to in-

123. Id. at 816.
124. Id. at 762.
125. See, e.g., Lujan v. Defenders of Wildlife, 112 S.Ct. 2130 (1992), and discussion at pp. 30–32 above.

tentionally deprecate people because of their religion or is undertaken for the arguably questionable purpose of accommodating mainstream religions.[126] But however persuasive these criticisms may be, they are greatly mitigated when the state action has wholly legitimate purposes and consequences.

Several Supreme Court decisions in this area have held that abstract objections or "atmospheric burdens"[127] rather than more tangible injuries are not legally cognizable. For example, in *Lyng v. Northwest Indian Cemetery Protective Association,* American Indians sought to prevent the United States Forest Service from building a road through a section of a national forest that they had historically used for religious purposes, because completion of the road would "virtually destroy the . . . Indians' ability to practice their religion."[128] The Court declined to apply heightened scrutiny, distinguishing between, on the one hand, the "incidental effects" of the government's conduct of its own internal affairs (such as laying highways) and, on the other hand, the government's "penalizing" or "coercing" persons for taking religiously motivated actions (by making them criminal) or "inducing" individuals to engage in or refrain from activity demanded by their faith (by denying civil benefits). The Court reasoned that the Free Exercise Clause "simply cannot be understood to require the Government to conduct its own internal affairs in ways that comport with the religious beliefs of particular citizens."[129] Even though "indirect coercion or penalties on the free exercise of religion, not just outright prohibitions, are subject to scrutiny under the First Amendment,"[130] the Court adopted a different approach for review of government regulations that use neither carrots nor sticks to affect religious interests.

Although the *Lyng* decision contained other elements that

126. Id.
127. Ira C. Lupu, Where Rights Begin: The Problems of Burdens on the Free Exercise of Religion, 102 Harv. L. Rev. 933, 987 (1989).
128. 485 U.S. 439, 451 (1988).
129. Id. at 448.
130. Id. at 450.

may explain its result,[131] the Court should not have been so restrictive in recognizing a real injury when it existed.[132] Another forceful illustration of the judiciary's declining to acknowledge genuine damage to religious faith may be found in a widely publicized ruling during the late 1980s that "mere exposure" to ideas presented in public school textbooks was not enough to bring the Free Exercise Clause into play, despite the belief of religious fundamentalists that their children would be eternally damned if they read the materials.[133] This was not just an occasion of discomfort or distress felt by those whose beliefs fell outside the mainstream of religious thought. Rather, these students were confronted with the choice of having the precepts of their faith abridged unless they either suffered the penalties of not complying with the regulations of the public school or paid the price of attending a private school.

Nor should the Court attempt to measure the scope of a given burden and the resulting amount of pressure it places on activities mandated or forbidden by religious doctrine. Judicial inquiry into such matters as how important a specific religious tenet is for a believer or how severely the government-imposed burden affects a particular individual's adherence to religious precepts places the courts in an undesirably intrusive posture.[134] It empowers judges to interpret value-laden theological principles and to assess essentially unquantifiable degrees of religious commitment, thus presenting far more opportunities for undesirable subjectivity or bias than when, for example, courts ask whether adherents have a good

131. See p. 90 below.
132. For other instances in which the Court has been unduly restrictive, see Choper, 70 Neb. L. Rev. at 667–68.
133. Mozert v. Hawkins County Board of Education, 827 F.2d 1058 (6th Cir. 1987).
134. For similar reasons, the Court should not pursue the suggestion of several opinions that it consider whether a "cardinal principle" or a "central" tenet of the individual's religious beliefs is involved. See Sherbert v. Verner, 374 U.S. 398, 406 (1963); Lyng, 485 U.S. at 474 (Brennan, J., dissenting).

faith belief that noncompliance with a precept of their faith carries extratemporal consequences. Finally, to balance the considerations just described against the strength of the government interest involves a weighing of incommensurables that creates even more serious problems of judicial prerogative in constitutional adjudication.

Nonetheless, the burdensome effect principle does adopt the basic criterion of some threshold injury to the free exercise of religion. It requires consequences greater than offended sensibilities produced by religiously grounded objections to government action. In an especially clear example, *Tony and Susan Alamo Foundation v. Secretary of Labor*,[135] the tenets of a nonprofit religious organization forbade receipt of the federal minimum wage by its "associates" (employees). The Court found no "actual burden,"[136] that is, no genuine injury, interpreting the Fair Labor Standards Act as permitting the organization to continue compensating workers with food, clothing, shelter, and other benefits rather than cash wages. Moreover, "even if the Foundation were to pay wages in cash, or if the associates' beliefs precluded them from accepting the statutory amount, there is nothing in the Act [nor, apparently, in the tenets of the religious group],[137] to prevent the associates from returning the amounts to the Foundation, provided that they do so voluntarily."[138]

EXEMPTION ONLY

In all cases where the Court found a Free Exercise Clause violation under the doctrine that governed before *Smith*,[139]

135. 471 U.S. 290 (1985).
136. Id. at 303.
137. See id. at 304 n. 29.
138. Id. at 304.
139. See Wisconsin v. Yoder, 406 U.S. 205 (1972) (state must exempt Amish children from requirement of school attendance until age sixteen); Sherbert v. Verner, 374 U.S. 398 (1963) (state cannot deny unemployment compensation to person for not accepting "suitable work" when the job required her to work on the Sabbath day of her faith); Thomas v. Review Board, 450 U.S. 707 (1980) (same); Hobbie v. Unemployment Appeals Commission, 480 U.S. 136 (1987) (same); Frazee v. Illinois Department of

the challengers simply sought exemptions for themselves, requiring the government to make limited accommodations in
the pursuit of its objectives. In *Lyng,* by contrast, the Native
Americans wanted the government to abandon altogether the
route for the roadway it intended to build.[140] In practice, the
Court has granted remedies that would force the government
to eliminate an entire program only when the assailed government action has sought to advance religion,[141] as in the
school prayer cases.[142]

The matter is not uncomplicated, especially in respect to
characterizing action as "abandonment" rather than "exemption." For example, one might well question the degree of
difference between the remedies of requiring the government to build a road a few miles away from its preferred site
and requiring it to exempt certain individuals from a general
program like the military draft.[143] Nonetheless, in order to
restrict the policy-making role of judges when they engage
in constitutional adjudication and to limit the reach of the
burdensome effect principle, I urge adoption of a rule that
would preclude the judiciary from weighing or balancing the
effect of the breadth of the remedy on the government's interest. Under this approach, those free exercise claims seeking relief that would require the government to abandon its
program entirely should be structurally distinguished and
denied.

Employment Security, 489 U.S. 829 (1989) (same); Bowen v. Roy, 476 U.S.
at 716 (Blackmun, J., concurring in part); 728–32 (O'Connor, Brennan,
and Marshall, JJ., concurring in part and dissenting in part); 733 (White,
J., dissenting) (state cannot require that person provide a social security
number in order to get welfare benefits; dictum of five justices).

140. At the very least, the Forest Service would have had to construct
the proposed roadway over land "that circumnavigated the high country
altogether," 485 U.S. at 462 (1988) (Brennan, J., dissenting). Failing that,
it might simply have had to give up the plan for any passageway in the
general vicinity.

141. This type of state program is the subject of chapter 4.

142. Wallace v. Jaffree, 472 U.S. 38 (1985); Abington School District
v. Schempp, 374 U.S. 203 (1963); Engel v. Vitale, 370 U.S. 421 (1962).

143. See Williams & Williams, 76 Corn. L. Rev. at 906, 910.

SINCERELY HELD

The Court has consistently required that a religious belief—whether or not ascribed to any organized group—must be in "good faith" or sincerely held in order to be protected under any interpretation of the Free Exercise Clause[144] (or accorded a special privilege by federal statute).[145] This requisite is far from ideal. In its leading decision approving the good faith criterion, the Court held that the Free Exercise Clause barred submitting to the jury the question whether certain religious beliefs were true, reasoning that "religious experiences which are as real as life to some may be incomprehensible to others. . . . If one could be sent to jail because a jury in a hostile environment found those teachings false, little indeed would be left of religious freedom."[146] But as Justice Jackson argued in dissenting from the Court's sincerity precept, it is extremely difficult to "separate an issue as to what is believed from considerations as to what is believable. The most convincing proof that one believes his statements is to show that they have been true in his experience."[147] Since "it is a normal human reaction to be skeptical about the sincerity of a person who claims to hold unconventional beliefs," there is a real likelihood that any inquiry into "good faith" will promote "a subtle preference for claims readily understandable by . . . adherents of mainstream religion."[148]

These realities may well call for special rules on allocation of the burden of proof: for example, assigning the risk of nonpersuasion to the government once the claimant has come forward with a possibly credible explanation. But an approach that required the courts to apply the burdensome

144. United States v. Ballard, 322 U.S. 78, 84 (1944). See also Thomas, 450 U.S. at 716 ("The narrow function of a reviewing court . . . is to determine whether . . . petitioner terminated his work because of an honest conviction that such work was forbidden by his religion.")

145. United States v. Seeger, 380 U.S. 163 (1965).

146. Ballard, 322 U.S. at 86–87.

147. Id. at 92–93 (Jackson, J., dissenting).

148. Mark Tushnet, "Of Church and State and the Supreme Court": Kurland Revisited, 1989 Sup. Ct. Rev. 373, 382.

effect principle to any claim simply asserted to be "religious" would be plainly unsatisfactory. When coupled with that part of the principle requiring that the law's coverage be "necessary to a compelling state interest," it would result in wholesale exemption from permissible government regulations (particularly for persons who were cynical or dishonest). As I noted in the earlier discussion of the breadth of the definition to be accorded religion, to avoid this outcome the Court would inevitably adopt a substantive standard of judicial review that would be much too deferential to help the truly devout.

ALTERNATIVE BURDEN

The criterion to be discussed here is usually more practical than doctrinal and involves only very modest action by the Court. Nonetheless, without significantly diminishing the constitutional protection for religious liberty, it promises a marked reduction in the potential number of free exercise claims under the burdensome effect principle that would meaningfully interfere with the government's ordinary ability to regulate. Just as Congress has demanded that religious objectors to military duty engage in alternative forms of service, and state lawmaking bodies have required that Sabbatarians excused from Sunday closing laws refrain from business on their Sabbath rather than on Sunday, the Court should either suggest or require that an alternative burden be imposed on individuals who would otherwise qualify for religious exemptions.

The precise contours of the alternative burden, which should tend to satisfy the state's regulatory interests without coming into conflict with the person's religious tenets, would of course have to vary with differing contexts. But in this manner members of religious faiths would be relieved of pressures to violate their beliefs and would not markedly benefit from their religious scruples relative to others. As a practical matter, the Court might well recommend this technique when it would minimize incentives to file fraudulent claims or reduce impingement on the government program involved. As a doctrinal matter, the Court should mandate that this compensatory obligation be imposed when it would lessen the likelihood that a government exemption would create Establishment Clause problems by inducing people to adopt certain beliefs.[149]

LEVEL OF SCRUTINY

The final issue for consideration is the degree of scrutiny the Court should apply to a free exercise claim that meets all the criteria of the burdensome effect principle. In light of the substantial narrowing of the constitutional right caused by satisfying all the other parts of the test and the consequent force of the claim for special protection, I would urge adoption of "strict" scrutiny—the government interest in not granting an exemption must be necessary to a compelling interest. This is a particularly appropriate measure when compared with other existing levels of review.

The "rational basis" standard—denial of an exemption need only be rationally related to a constitutionally permissible state goal—may be easily rejected because it affords no greater protection than the Due Process Clause already grants against government interference with any "liberty" or "property" interest; thus it deprives the Free Exercise Clause of any independent force.

A conventional "balancing" approach—in which the Court weighs the strength of the state interest against the burden on religious exercise—is deficient, in my view, for several reasons. First, as I noted above, this enterprise involves a comparison of incommensurables that creates serious problems of judicial prerogative in constitutional adjudication; I believe it should be avoided at most costs. Although it must be conceded, as we shall see again shortly, that no measure of judicial oversight (including the one I propose here)

149. As I noted at the outset of this chapter, one of the circumstances qualifying the burdensome effect principle is that a judicially granted exemption under the Free Exercise Clause must not violate the Establishment Clause. This final criterion will be discussed at length in chapter 4 and, as we shall see, constitutes a substantial limitation on the scope of the right.

can wholly avoid the use of political-policy criteria by courts, still the difference in degree of opportunity for such judgments between a straightforward process of interest balancing and the test of strict scrutiny is so great as to effectively amount to a difference in kind.

Second, this problem of legislature-like judgments by the judicial branch would probably be exacerbated, as was also discussed earlier, by the range of free exercise claims that would potentially come to the courts under the burdensome effect principle (even as circumscribed by the need to have all its elements met). Those challenges would probably involve a broader number of government policies than would arise in connection with any other personal constitutional right.[150]

Finally, a particular problem with judicial balancing is that it is "susceptible to overt and, even more important, unconscious manipulation."[151] This is especially threatening in respect to religious liberty and the burdensome effect principle. The risk is that a balancing approach "will be administered with a thumb on the scales—or with a hand underneath the scale—when non-mainstream claims are made. The reason is that the less familiar the claim is—that is, the less connected it is to the kinds of worship that the Justices of the Supreme Court are accustomed to—the less likely it is that they will regard infringements on those forms of worship as really serious. The Justices may of course say that they assume that the claims of severe impairment are both sincere and accurate, but there is some distance between saying that and believing it in a way that finds expression in the application of a balancing test."[152]

It has been noted that strict scrutiny is "strict in theory but fatal in fact."[153] This is surely true when the standard is applied with integrity, in undiluted form. There are exceedingly few government programs that may fairly be described

---

150. See pp. 61–63 above.

151. Tushnet, 1989 Sup. Ct. Rev. at 382.

152. Id. at 383.

153. Gerald Gunther, In Search of Evolving Doctrine on a Changing Court: A Model for a Newer Equal Protection, 86 Harv. L. Rev. 1, 8 (1972).

as overwhelmingly necessary, and fewer still that a court could straightforwardly find must be implemented *without exception* (as would be the case in regard to the burdensome effect principle).[154] Thus adoption of the strict scrutiny standard of review would mean that virtually all claims—but not *all*, as we shall see in a moment—for a Free Exercise Clause exemption that survive the qualifying hurdles of the burdensome effect principle would ultimately be successful.

Most cases will be easy to decide. For example, if a student seeks relief from a school's uniform dress policy for gym class because her religious beliefs forbid her to wear an immodest costume;[155] or if an individual considers the photograph on a driver's license a graven image forbidden by the Second Commandment;[156] or if the religious tenets of an Amish buggy driver bar compliance with a state law requiring that slow-moving vehicles display a special emblem;[157] then exemptions should be granted. The government has only the most limited interest in forcing religious objectors to conform to such regulations. Indeed, if the record shows that religious

154. Analysis of how the strict scrutiny test might be refined beyond its broadly stated criteria is beyond the scope of this book. In my view, though, there is much to commend the Court's asking the following question as one step in assessing the actual significance of the state regulation: "Is the governmental interest so important that the government would impose a burden of this magnitude on the majority in order to achieve it?" McConnell, 57 U. Chi. L. Rev. at 1147. For analogous formulations in respect to related issues, see Eric Schnapper, Two Categories of Discriminatory Intent, 17 Harv. C.R.–C.L. L. Rev. 31 (1982); David A. Strauss, Discriminatory Intent and the Taming of Brown, 56 U. Chi. L. Rev. 935 (1989). Careful application of this formulation would ensure that minority religious groups not be subjected to curtailment of their religious freedom simply because they lack the influence that mainstream groups can bring to bear upon the legislative process, and would probably result in upholding the free exercise claim in most instances. It should be noted, in addition, that an affirmative answer does not necessarily lead to the conclusion that accomplishment of the government's objective demands that no exemption be given to a (small) *minority*.

155. See Mitchell v. McCall, 273 Ala. 604, 143 So.2d 629 (1962), discussed at pp. 21–22 above.

156. Quaring v. Peterson, 728 F.2d 1121 (8th Cir. 1984), aff'd by equally divided court sub nom., Jensen v. Quaring, 472 U.S. 478 (1985).

157. State v. Hershberger, 462 N.W.2d 393 (Minn. 1990).

exceptions to particular government rules have often (or even sometimes) been legislatively granted in different jurisdictions over various periods,[158] this should be persuasive evidence that the state's interest is insufficient to deny a judicially compelled exemption. By contrast, overriding government concerns are plainly implicated when, even for religious reasons, parents neglect to provide any medical care for serious health needs of their children, or a school bus driver believes in child sacrifice,[159] or substance abuse counselors refuse to abstain from using drugs themselves despite their obvious status as role models for their dependent clients. Any special exemptions in such circumstances should be denied.

Other cases might be considered less readily soluble. When, as in *Yoder,* an individual's religion forbids attending high school; or when, as in *Smith,* a person seeks to use mind-altering drugs for sacramental purposes; or when, as in *Bob Jones University v. United States,*[160] an organization's religious precepts require discrimination on the basis of race (or sex), one may fairly debate whether the government has a sufficiently strong interest at stake. Yet because of the bedrock nature of the claim if all the barriers of the burdensome effect principle are overcome, and given the degree of imposition on religious liberty—a constitutional right whose textual, historical, and contemporary credentials are equaled by few others—I believe the level of scrutiny urged here should result in free exercise vindication even in these situations.

158. See chapter 4, note 39 below.
159. See Hollon v. Pierce, 257 Cal. App.2d 468, 64 Cal. Rptr. 808 (1967).
160. 461 U.S. 574 (1983). This decision is considered further under other elements of my proposed thesis at pp. 131–32 below.

4

....

Intentional Advantage Principle

Government programs that deliberately favor religious interests or government actions that relieve individuals because of their religious beliefs from the burdens of generally applicable regulations should be held to violate the Establishment Clause only if the programs or actions pose a significant threat to religious liberty or if they are discriminatory.

As analogously observed in connection with the deliberate disadvantage principle, there is an important distinction between a lawmaking body's setting out to give an "advantage" to—or, in alphabetical order, to "advance," "aid," "assist," "benefit," "favor," "help," "sponsor," or "support"—a religious cause and state action that is concededly taken to further legitimate public welfare ends but is in some part traceable to the religious affiliation, ideals or values (or other ideological tenets) of members of the legislature. The "intentional advantage" principle concerns action of the first kind and requires examination of the lawmakers' motivations in an effort to ascertain what they hoped to accomplish through the operation of their enactment. Since the principle makes such action more constitutionally vulnerable than action in the second category (or than action undertaken for truly mixed motives),[1] this may encourage attempts to cloak it. Thus it is necessary to fix guidelines that will make action

1. This "third" category covers situations in which many lawmakers wish to accomplish either both ends or one of the two ends, rather than legislating simply to achieve ordinary policy goals. Regulations prohibiting abortion and providing aid to parochial schools strike me as especially good examples. The second and third types of action will be considered in connection with the "independent impact" principle in chapter 5.

falling under the intentional advantage principle readily identifiable.

In a significant sense, all government action that deliberately favors religious interests may be fairly described as an "accommodation" for religion: either for one or more of the nation's mainstream religious groups or for religious minorities. Perhaps because such undertakings are not seen as being so hostile to deeply held national values as are deliberate attempts to prejudice persons because of their religious beliefs, most legal enactments that favor religion do so plainly by their terms—for example, a statutory military draft exemption for religious objectors or a city's display of a Latin cross on public property—and pose no problems of going behind the face of the law to discover motivation. Periodically, however, there are more subtle (or even concealed) efforts, either making no mention of religion at all or, more often, seeking to characterize (or subsequently defend) as nonsectarian an activity that is generally understood as having only a religious basis.[2]

INQUIRY INTO MOTIVE

In contrast to unstated purposeful discrimination against religious minorities, which occurs very rarely, "intentional advantage" situations (especially in support of mainstream religions) arise frequently. Fortunately, though, as with instances of deliberate discrimination, the suspicious appearance of intentional advantage programs will ordinarily be quite clear even if wrapped in the verbal cellophane of the secular public welfare. Indeed, in the discussion of the relative ease of discerning motivation under the deliberate disadvantage principle, all of the illustrations from the religion area, in contrast to the racial sphere, grew out of government attempts to *favor* religion, mostly involving the public schools: Bible reading

2. For example, assume that the school board of an overwhelmingly Catholic community explained its requirement that the catechism be taught to all first-graders in the public schools as a technique to develop memory skills.

and prayer (vocal and silent), the teaching of evolution and creation science, and posting the Ten Commandments in classrooms. In addition, several cases concerning government acknowledgment of religion—legislative prayers by chaplains, and the display of crèches and menorahs on public property—present activities that may be readily categorized as purposefully meant to benefit religion. Occasional assertions by some justices to the contrary notwithstanding,[3] the straightforward assessment of most members of the Court comports with the general public perception of these practices' obvious religious intent and, as under the deliberate disadvantage principle, makes the delicate inquiry of determining what the lawmaking body really hoped to accomplish a manageable task under the intentional advantage principle as well. Finally, even if the judiciary misreads the reality and erroneously concludes that the lawmaking body did not seek to achieve an end in favor of religion, that does not fully remove the cloud of possible unconstitutionality. Rather, as we shall see under the "independent impact" principle in chapter 5, government action whose *effect* is to benefit religion may also be invalid under the Establishment Clause.

RATIONALE FOR ACCOMMODATIONS

The judicial search for legislative and administrative motivation is of greater urgency for purposes of the deliberate disadvantage principle than for the intentional advantage precept. As set forth more fully in chapter 2, purposeful discrimination against members of minority religious (or racial) groups conflicts with our most fundamental values, is especially illicit (almost per se invalid) as a matter of present con-

---

3. See, e.g., Lynch v. Donnelly, 465 U.S. at 680–81 (crèche has "legitimate secular purposes": "depicts the historical origins" of Christmas); id. at 691 (O'Connor, J., concurring) (crèche has "legitimate secular purpose": "celebration of the public holiday through its traditional symbols"); Allegheny County v. ACLU, 492 U.S. at 613–16 (Blackmun, J., announcing judgment of the Court) (display of Christmas tree and menorah "simply recognizes that both Christmas and Chanukah are part of the same winter-holiday season").

stitutional doctrine as well as under my thesis, and therefore justifies extraordinary efforts for detection. In contrast, intentional *advantage* for religion is more benign, both as a matter of historical tradition and as a subject of contemporary concern.

It has the most widespread support—that of orthodox liberal separationists like Justice Brennan and advocates of the endorsement approach like Justice O'Connor, as well as that of conventional deferential conservatives like Justice Scalia (although not that of the adherents of the neutrality approach)—when the state grants special consideration to minority religions by excusing them from broad government regulations that burden them because of the tenets of their faith (such as most jurisdictions did with peyote for the Native American Church). Much of this approbation weakens, however (and is already unavailable from neutralists), when the majority-dominated political process seeks to help mainstream religions. Although many church-state theorists will continue to accept government efforts to alleviate a burden imposed by a generally applicable law (such as the exemption for religion—read Christianity and Judaism—during Prohibition), a good deal of support dissipates when the state goes beyond mitigating problems created by government and more affirmatively seeks to "accommodate" the religiously grounded desires of large numbers of citizens (such as by Christmas—or Christmas/Chanukah—displays).

DIFFERENCES BETWEEN RELIGION AND RACE

The intentional advantage principle generally permits the state to act on behalf of religious interests or beliefs. This reflects the value judgment that it is worthwhile for government to acknowledge the feelings of members of mainstream religions about "their most central values and concerns" by responding to their wishes not to be "excluded from a public culture devoted purely to secular concerns,"[4] and that these

4. Steven D. Smith, Symbols, Perceptions, and Doctrinal Illusions: Establishment Neutrality and the "No Endorsement" Test, 86 Mich. L. Rev.

"accommodations" should survive constitutional attack unless they pose a meaningful threat to religious liberty. Although deliberately *disadvantaging* individuals because of their religion is the constitutional and moral equivalent of invidiously discriminating against people because of their race, contemporary American experience indicates that there are significant differences between race and religion when deliberate *advantage* is at issue. Government action that intentionally confers a benefit on the racial majority concomitantly prejudices racial minorities. For example, exempting whites from a rule against serving alcoholic beverages to minors, or making public property available to celebrate the Confederacy, ordinarily treats nonwhites with a tangible disrespect by denying a meaningful privilege or conveying a message of racial insensitivity that is generally not present when analogous action benefits mainstream religions. The contention that "a favorable statement about one class is not necessarily a correlative pejorative remark about another class,"[5] is *not* true in the racial examples just given, although it will frequently be valid in a religious context. Thus, though I agree that "when government displays the symbols of the dominant religion—as when government displays the symbols of white supremacy—the pain is not distributed evenly,"[6] I do *not* believe that the message sent to religious minorities is in any meaningful way as hurtful and offensive as it is to racial minorities. This is probably true in part because the substantive precepts of both

---

266, 311 (1987); see also Arlin M. Adams & Charles J. Emmerich, A Heritage of Religious Liberty, 137 U. Pa. L. Rev. 1559, 1616 (1989): "[T]he Founders affirmed the importance of religion to the new republic and would have rejected the use of the establishment clause to eradicate the religious leaven from public life. Instead, while recognizing the historical dangers posed by religious establishments, they would agree that government may acknowledge the crucial importance of religion to many citizens."

5. William P. Marshall, The Concept of Offensiveness in Establishment and Free Exercise Jurisprudence, 66 Ind. L.J. 351, 365 (1991). See chapter 1, note 134 above.

6. Kenneth L. Karst, The First Amendment, the Politics of Religion and the Symbols of Government, 27 Harv. C.R.–C.L. L. Rev. 503, 511 (1992).

mainstream and minority faiths (such as the golden rule or most of the Ten Commandments) are often perceived as containing special value for the secular welfare of society. As a consequence, it is possible that favor or support for some religions may be viewed as public recognition of certain appealing beliefs or appreciation for various beneficial activities rather than merely an indirect expression of disrespect toward "nonpreferred" religions. The overtones of racial prejudice and intolerance historically associated with messages of, for example, white supremacy are simply not present. Thus, favoring the dominant racial group should be (and is) almost always invalid, whereas assisting mainstream religious groups need not be forbidden, in my judgment, unless it adversely affects religious liberty. In contrast to our national ideal and ultimate goal that a person's race should be irrelevant to decision making by government officials and interaction with private citizens, our heritage has positively approved of the flourishing of religious freedom and respected the spiritual concerns of the individual, traditionally recognizing that "religion is a source of many good things—insight, guidance, inspiration, comfort, and more"[7] for many people, and affirming the unique contribution of religious institutions to the pluralism of American society.

Furthermore, an important part of the rationale for the burdensome effect principle also lends support to the intentional advantage principle's permitting favorable treatment for mainstream religions. The primary thrust of the burdensome effect principle is to grant a special immunity for minority religions under the Free Exercise Clause that is not afforded to minority racial/ethnic groups under the Equal Protection Clause. The reasoning that undergirds this result leads to the similarly disparate treatment of race and religion urged by the intentional advantage principle. A major explanation for empowering the courts to mandate a religious ex-

7. Gary J. Simson, Laws Intentionally Favoring Mainstream Religions: An Unhelpful Comparison to Race, 79 Corn. L. Rev. 514, 519 (1993).

emption from generally applicable laws lay in recognizing the sensitive consideration given in the political process to the desires of mainstream religions, either because they actually comprise a majority bloc on some matters or, more often, because their support is essential in assembling the coalition of minorities needed to govern. Judicial protection is therefore needed for minority religions to restore some degree of influence in securing their constitutional right to religious freedom, power that was already possessed by mainstream religions in the lawmaking system. Justifying use of the Court's authority for minority religions by pointing to the normal political force held by mainstream religions acknowledges the actual use and legitimacy of that lawmaking power. It follows, in my view, that this legislative advantage for mainstream religions should be permitted—even when it extends beyond exemptions from generally applicable rules—in the absence of a meaningful threat to religious liberty.

DEFINITION OF "RELIGIOUS" INTERESTS OR BELIEFS

The intentional advantage principle triggers special constitutional attention to state action that favors or benefits "religious" interests or beliefs. This raises the issue of how to define religion for this purpose. The distinctive reasons for constructing a restrictive definition for the burdensome effect principle, which concerned an immunity for *conduct* demanded or forbidden by religious tenets, do not apply here. Indeed, if the intentional advantage principle were to reach only ideologies concerning extratemporal consequences, a wide variety of activities that are generally regarded as religious (despite the absence of any afterlife connection) could be aided or sponsored by the state free of my thesis's strictures against threats to religious liberty. To illustrate, the public schools might have voluntary programs of prayers to God seeking only worldly assistance, or state funds might be granted to a modern Protestant sect whose beliefs excluded salvation or related eternal matters. As with the deliberate disadvantage principle, that the government assistance under consideration here is being afforded to groups or people because of their *beliefs* or *associations* with others calls for a much more inclusive definition.

For example, although it is (and should be) within a state's constitutional authority to offer a public school program in meditation for the purpose of teaching students psychologically beneficial techniques of concentration and relaxation, this should be contrasted with a litigated New Jersey public school course in transcendental meditation (and the related "science of creative intelligence"). The federal court's review of the contents of the textbook found that the "creative intelligence" it described was analogous to the broad concept of "God" used by modern theologians.[8] The court also concluded that the "puja," a ceremony in which each student received a mantra with which to meditate,[9] was an invocation of a deified human being.[10] Therefore the course was "nothing more than an effort to propagate TM, SCI and the views of Maharishi Makesh Yogi"[11]—an attempt by government "to encourage this version of ultimate truth."[12] Even if the "ultimate truth" promoted by the public school did not invoke any extratemporal consequences, such ideological partisanship by government that would be commonly perceived as "religious" should readily fall within the intentional advantage principle's definition of religion.

But what of other systems of belief? For example, there is no constitutional difficulty with a public school's offering courses in morality or philosophy—just as "study of the Bible or of religion, when presented objectively as part of a secular program of education,"[13] is fully permissible. However, I think that the state's attempt (through its schools or otherwise) to convince its people (through either its regulatory or

8. Malnak v. Yogi, 440 F. Supp. 1284, 1321–22 (D.N.J. 1977) aff'd, 592 F.2d 197 (3d Cir. 1979).

9. Id. at 1289–1312.

10. Id. at 1323.

11. Malnak v. Yogi, 592 F.2d 197, 215 (3d Cir. 1979) (Adams, J., concurring).

12. Id. at 214.

13. Abington School District v. Schempp, 374 U.S. 203, 225 (1963).

its fiscal powers) of the "ultimate truth" of the teachings of
Dewey or Hegel—or Keynes or Friedman, or Luther or
Christ—should be treated no differently for constitutional
purposes from government's effort to persuade its citizens of
the correctness of traditionally "religious" systems of belief
such as Deism, Protestantism, or Yoga.[14] As was seen in the
earlier discussion of the complexities of defining religion, the
dividing line between theologically grounded ideologies and
those commonly considered to be based on secular premises
is exceedingly dim, if discernible at all. Although government
may undoubtedly regulate the *conduct* of its citizens in order
to promote society's perception of the public welfare despite
such programs' having emanated from dogmatic ideological
roots (whether religious or otherwise), and though public officials must be able to inform and educate the people, it is an
entirely different matter for the state to commit its collective
resources to persuade its people to *believe* in the validity of
certain ideas.[15] But how does the specific issue under discussion—articulating a definition of religion for purposes of the
Establishment Clause's bar on undue advantage to religion—
relate to this broader problem?

14. If government attempts to avoid ideological indoctrination by presenting ideas "objectively as part of a secular program of education," id., it
may be fairly contended that this is a morally relativistic stance that itself
represents a particular sectarian position: "value neutrality itself has a value
bias favoring the liberal philosophy embodied by the scientific method of
inquiry." Stanley Ingber, Religious Children and the Inevitable Compulsion
of Public Schools, 43 Case W. L. Rev. 773, 779 (1993). For example, "if
schools attempt to avoid exerting influence upon the students' attitudes,
children may perceive an indifferent approach to various moral options by
the adult authority as indicating the intrinsic equality of all options and
the arbitrariness of choosing among them. Schools, then, are accused of
encouraging a hedonistic—anything goes—attitude." Id. at 774 n. 6. But
if government was precluded from pursuing this alternative, then it would
be literally impossible for the state to engage in any informational or educational function.

15. "The ideology of democratic government posits the existence of
autonomous citizens who make informed and intelligent judgments about
government policies, free of a state preceptorship that substantially impedes
individual choice and consent by selective transmission of information."
Mark G. Yudof, When Government Speaks: Politics, Law, and Government
Expression in America 32 (1983).

Other Constitutional Provisions

The strongest promise for a workable solution lies in constitutional provisions other than the Religion Clauses, and therefore a definition of religion for the intentional advantage principle need not be developed further. The freedom of expression and association guarantees of the First Amendment have been interpreted to impose significant, albeit as yet sketchily defined, limitations on the government's ability to support, or require its citizens to support, particular beliefs or groups, whether or not their teachings or tenets are generally considered to be "religious."[16] But "there is no political establishment clause"; "in the context of political speech, there is virtually no First Amendment limit on what the government may say."[17] Thus, under present doctrine there is no strict constitutional requirement "that government must be ideologically 'neutral.'"[18] It may be assumed that, at a minimum, those who disdain American patriotic symbols have no constitutional right to "prevent government from promoting respect for the flag by proclaiming Flag Day or by using public property to display the flag . . . [or by spending] public funds to subsidize flag production."[19] Moreover, it would seem that "'Just say no to drugs,' 'End Racism,' and 'Have babies, not abortions' are all messages government is free to endorse under current law."[20]

16. Wooley v. Maynard, 430 U.S. 705 (1977) (state may not require use of license plates with display of motto to which vehicle owner is ideologically opposed); Abood v. Detroit Board of Education, 431 U.S. 209 (1977) ("service charges" required of public employees may not be spent by union for ideological causes opposed by employee); Keller v. State Bar of California, 496 U.S. 1 (1990) (same in re lawyers' compulsory dues to state bar association); West Virginia State Board of Education v. Barnette, 319 U.S. 624 (1943) (public school pupils may not be required to salute American flag).

17. Kathleen M. Sullivan, Religion and Liberal Democracy, 59 U. Chi. L. Rev. 195, 206 (1992), citing Meese v. Keene, 481 U.S. 465 (1987) (government may require that advocacy materials produced by or under the aegis of a foreign government be labeled "political propaganda").

18. Laurence H. Tribe, American Constitutional Law 804 (2d ed. 1988).

19. Id. at 807.

20. Sullivan, 59 U. Chi. L. Rev. at 207.

Nonetheless, although it is true that "the Court has never applied or even seriously entertained applying the principle [of no government-compelled support of ideological causes] to the tax system," neither reason nor authority makes it "clear that the tax system has a bye"[21] in respect to these matters. It may be conceded that the solution to such thorny constitutional problems as the extent to which government may underwrite political speech, artistic expression, or the education of children in respect to values is exceedingly complicated and still at or beyond the frontiers of developing First Amendment principles. Similarly, it must be acknowledged—as the extended discussion of defining religion in chapter 3 reveals—that any effort to draw a reasoned line between "religious" beliefs (which may not be supported by the state under existing law and would come under the intentional advantage principle) and "nonreligious" ideologies (which may be furthered by the government) is extraordinarily difficult if not impossible. Still, there is every reason to believe that government efforts to subsidize or promote such narrow partisan ideologies as the school prayers to God or the aid to modern Protestant sects hypothesized above—to fund these activities, or to attempt to indoctrinate citizens in these views, or to persuade them to accept these beliefs— would, apart from the Establishment Clause, abridge the freedom of association's ban on requiring a person "to contribute to the support of an ideological cause he may oppose"[22] and invade "the sphere of intellect and spirit which it is the purpose of the First Amendment to our Constitution to reserve from all official control."[23]

This does not lead inevitably to the conclusion that the Constitution forbids all references to, or even all endorsements of, religious or other narrow partisan ideologies by government or its officials. It is one thing for the president of the United States to declare that he believes in God or that

---

21. Id. at 210.
22. Abood, 431 U.S. at 235.
23. Barnette, 319 U.S. at 642.

he prays that the Ruler of the Universe will watch over our nation, or even to urge that all citizens respect and seek inspiration from a supreme being. Abraham Lincoln's renowned Second Inaugural Address has been described as "a moving, theologically inspired meditation on the ways of human sin and redemption and of divine providence and retribution."[24] These views are expressions of the public officer as an individual who does not forfeit his constitutional right to speak his mind and talk from his heart. Even if we could connect some portion of his government salary with this activity—an allocation I do not believe can realistically be made—the amount would undoubtedly be de minimis. Indeed, even if Congress were to finance the inscription of the Second Inaugural on a wall of the Lincoln Memorial, that would be to honor the author rather than to adopt his thoughts as the law of the land. It is, however, another thing altogether for government to articulate and sponsor Lincoln's message as an official view, as when New Hampshire required that all car license plates display the partisan ideological motto "Live Free or Die."[25] This the provisions of the First Amendment—speech, association, or religion—should interdict. Ultimately, the solution to the constitutional problem, and the challenge to First Amendment theorists, is to develop a coherent doctrine that meaningfully distinguishes what I have loosely described as "narrow partisan ideologies" (which government may not subsidize or promote) from what may conclusorily be labeled as "widely shared and basically noncontroversial public values," such as the inherent dignity of the individual and the essential equality of all human beings (which the state may be thought able to aid or sponsor).

American Civil Religion

The contours of the problem may be illuminated by examining the idea that certain kinds of official pronounce-

---

24. Yehudah Mirsky, Civil Religion and the Establishment Clause, 95 Yale L.J. 1237, 1238 (1986).
25. Wooley, note 16 above.

ments that most people would consider on first thought to be "religious" precepts are really not so at all. Rather, on further reflection these declarations are revealed as secular, political statements that fall within the category of "widely shared and basically noncontroversial public values" and are thus outside the intentional advantage principle.

This broad proposition draws heavily on Robert Bellah's concept of an American "civil religion"[26] (which may in turn have some roots in Benjamin Franklin's notion of a "public religion").[27] One version of the thought has been expressed in Supreme Court opinions during recent years under the title "ceremonial deism."[28] Although there is no clearly developed definition of "civil religion" generally agreed upon by those who have sought to employ it in the service of the constitutional separation of church and state,[29] there are some commonly understood elements that distinguish it from "traditional religion."

The concept of American civil religion begins with a set of widely shared values that are often invoked to solemnize and elevate public rituals and ceremonies. These beliefs are theistic in that they acknowledge the existence of God but are nonsectarian within that framework in that the conception of God is different from that of any particular religion. "Though much is selectively derived from Christianity, this religion is

26. Robert N. Bellah, Civil Religion in America, 96 Daedalus 1 (winter 1967).

27. See Martin E. Marty, Pilgrims in Their Own Land: 500 Years of Religion in America 154–66 (1984).

28. Lynch, 465 U.S. at 716 (Brennan, J., dissenting); Allegheny County, 492 U.S. at 630 (O'Connor, J., concurring in part).

29. The difference between a general theory and its specific application may be sharply illustrated by the fact that the two principal law review pieces on the subject of civil religion come to opposite conclusions with regard to the practice of a legislature's paying a minister to open each of its sessions with a prayer. Mirsky, 95 Yale L.J. at 1244 n. 37 (invalid); Michael M. Maddigan, The Establishment Clause, Civil Religion, and the Public Church, 81 Calif. L. Rev. 293, 337–38 (1993) (valid). The question also divided Justices Blackmun and O'Connor (valid) from Justices Brennan, Marshall, and Stevens (invalid) in Marsh v. Chambers, 463 U.S. 783 (1983).

clearly not itself Christianity. . . . The God of the civil religion is not only rather 'unitarian,' he is also on the austere side, much more related to order, law, and right than to salvation and love. Even though he is somewhat deist in cast, he is by no means simply a watchmaker God."[30] Further, it does not address what most preoccupies traditional religions— separating the sacred (good) from the profane (bad). Instead, its central message is peculiarly patriotic: "God has uniquely blessed America and will assure its prosperity if it is virtuous."[31] America is the "chosen nation": "the city upon a hill, an idealized version of the United States, the United States as it could be at its best."[32] This set of images and values, it is said, has become assimilated into American culture, fostering "a unified, cohesive sense of social identity for all members of the polity."[33] Indeed, to avoid a confusion in terms, it might better be defined as a "civil mythology," to be contrasted with a "theological religion," which is the major concern of the Religion Clauses.[34]

An intelligent argument has been made that the practices of American civil religion are sufficiently secular and patriotic not to be encompassed by the intentional advantage principle's caution against favoring or benefiting religion. It is important to note at the outset that this would not mean that these customs are fully immune from judicial review under the Religion Clauses. Pursuant to the burdensome effect principle, the Free Exercise Clause may require an exemption from secular government action that conflicts with religious tenets. Even if one accepts the proposition that our civil religion is consciously "nonsectarian" in furtherance of the

30. Robert N. Bellah, Beyond Belief: Essays on Religion in a Post-Traditional World 175 (1970).
31. Maddigan, 81 Calif. L. Rev. at 323.
32. Id. at 326.
33. Mirsky, 95 Yale L.J. at 1256.
34. Interestingly, Justice Brennan's acceptance of practices of "ceremonial deism" as beyond constitutional purview is more limited and grudging: "they have lost through rote repetition any significant religious content." Lynch, 465 U.S. at 716 (Brennan, J., dissenting).

American ideal of religious tolerance,[35] not only will its invocation of God surely cause it to be viewed as religious by some observers, but in many contexts it will impose burdens sufficient to qualify for consideration of a constitutionally compelled exemption (e.g., from attendance at some public ritual).

The major difference in a government action's falling under the intentional advantage principle rather than the burdensome effect principle involves the remedy. If the practice meaningfully interferes with religious liberty, the former principle requires the program's total elimination. But if the practice meets the requisites of the latter principle, only an exemption is required: even though the conflict with religious beliefs imposed by a *secular* regulation (say, a mandatory public school course in sex education) may be substantial enough to call for special treatment for religion,[36] societal needs dictate that the activity continue for others even though the context may still endanger religious freedom. To illustrate: merely permitting schoolchildren to be excused from the course in sex education if it conflicts with the tenets of their faith may not, because of peer pressure, result in their actually not attending the class. That imposition on religious exercise, however, should not be required to be paid (and is not), as we shall see, when the government acts for *religious* purposes rather than to achieve a public welfare good.

In my view, if a program of civil religion—such as the state's employment of a chaplain to begin each legislative day with a prayer in *Marsh v. Chambers,* or a middle school's invitation to a member of the clergy to deliver an invocation and benediction at its graduation in *Lee v. Weisman*—poses a meaningful threat to religious liberty, it should be completely forbidden. It is fundamentally ideological in nature rather than being a conventional welfare regulation, and its obvi-

---

35. See generally Maddigan, 81 Calif. L. Rev. at 309–28.
36. See Ware v. Valley Stream High School District, 75 N.Y.2d 114, 550 N.E.2d 420 (1989).

ously close ties to, and common roots with, theological religious beliefs in contrast to some widely shared and largely uncontroversial patriotic values should make it subject to the intentional advantage principle.

EQUAL TREATMENT

In General

We have seen that government discrimination against persons or groups because of their religious beliefs undermines a core value of the First Amendment by posing a meaningful threat to religious liberty. Therefore, although government accommodations for both mainstream and minority religions are not automatically invalid under the intentional advantage principle, they must still pass an equality test in order to survive. As the Court recently confirmed,[37] the majority-dominated legislative and administrative process should not constitutionally be permitted to take care of its politically influential religious constituencies without doing so for others who are similarly situated religiously though less powerful politically, particularly because of the real risk that legislative accommodations for religion "will turn more on political favoritism and influence than on judgments of constitutional entitlement or acute religious need."[38]

It is important to acknowledge, however, that legislatures have not been consistently callous or hostile to the plight of minority religions. Congress's recent passage of the Religious Freedom Restoration Act of 1993 is a particularly salient example of political solicitude for religious freedom. But this attitude is by no means unique. A number of decisions in which a constitutionally compelled accommodation under the Free Exercise Clause was sought because a state had declined to voluntarily grant an exemption have observed that many

37. Board of Education of Kiryas Joel Village School District v. Grumet, 114 S.Ct. 2481 (1994).
38. Ira C. Lupu, Reconstructing the Establishment Clause: The Case against Discretionary Accommodation of Religion, 140 U. Pa. L. Rev. 555, 602 (1991).

other jurisdictions had seen fit to excuse religious objectors.[39] Still, since it may be expected that "accommodations by state legislatures will 1) create a nonuniform pattern of special treatment for religious concerns; 2) present an aggravated risk of special treatment for religions dominant in particular states; and 3) create the further risk of invidiously omitted accommodations for those religions which are in disfavor,"[40] judicial superintendence of the rule of equality is strongly needed.

As evidenced by the division among the justices in the recent decision invalidating New York's creation of a special school district for the Satmar Hasidim,[41] what constitutes impermissible discrimination in this context requires further analysis. The reality is that a combination of the dynamics of the political process (just described) and the wide diversity of religious beliefs in our society makes it inevitable that government accommodations will result in some degree of differential treatment of religious faiths. In practice, the state will usually single out a particular religious tenet for special privilege—for example, required use of hallucinogenic drugs, forbidden attendance at certain public school courses, prohibited service on a jury. Each of these statutory exemptions may be seen as favoring the beneficiary religions over all others. Indeed, even more generally applicable immunities, such as

39. See, e.g., Employment Division v. Smith, 494 U.S. 872, 912–13 n. 5 (1990) (Blackmun, J., dissenting) (twenty-three states and the federal government had exempted the sacramental use of peyote from their criminal laws); Wisconsin v. Yoder, 406 U.S. 205, 208 n. 3 (1972) (four states had reached a "compromise settlement" with the Amish with respect to compulsory high school attendance); Braunfeld v. Brown, 366 U.S. 599, 614 (1961) (Brennan, J., concurring and dissenting) (twenty-one of thirty-four states with Sunday closing laws had exempted persons whose religions require a day of rest other than Sunday). Similarly, after the Court held in Goldman v. Weinberger, 475 U.S. 503 (1986), that the Free Exercise Clause did not require an exemption from an air force rule barring the wearing of headgear indoors for an Orthodox Jewish psychologist who wished to keep his yarmulke on while in uniform on duty at a military hospital, Congress granted relief. Pub. L. 100–180, sec. 508, 100th Cong., 1st sess. (1987).

40. Lupu, 140 U. Pa. L. Rev. at 605–6.

41. Board of Education of Kiryas Joel Village School District v. Grumet, 114 S.Ct. 2481 (1994).

tax exemption for property that is used for religious purposes, will have a disparate impact, benefiting those churches
whose faith includes grand edifices in contrast to religions
with no real estate at all. Unless we follow the neutrality approach, all these legislative enactments cannot be prohibited
by the First Amendment. As a matter of constitutional doctrine, this unevenness was precisely the effect of all the Supreme Court's own decisions requiring Free Exercise Clause
exemptions from government regulations of conduct.[42] As
a matter of practicality, forbidding them would "deny the
validity of *any* accommodations other than perhaps a law
requiring, in general terms, accommodation of all religious beliefs."[43] In addition, proscribing exemptions would
be inconsistent with much evidence in respect to original
intent.[44]

It is another matter, however, to permit accommodations
that treat "similarly situated" religious practices differently.
The critical issue, of course, is how the Court should deter-

42. See chapter 3, note 139 above.

43. Timothy L. Hall, Religion, Equality, and Difference, 65 Temp. L.
Rev. 1, 86 n. 406 (1992); see also Michael W. McConnell, Accommodation
of Religion, 60 Geo. Wash. L. Rev. 685, 707 (1992) ("It is only natural for
legislatures to address free exercise problems as they arise"); Mark Tushnet,
"Of Church and State and the Supreme Court": Kurland Revisited, 1989
Sup. Ct. Rev. 373, 394 ("any statutory accommodation of religion will have
that sort of disparate impact"). Thus Justice O'Connor's point in Estate of
Thornton v. Caldor, Inc., 472 U.S. 703, 711 (1985) (O'Connor, J., concurring), that a state law accommodating beliefs regarding work on a Sabbath
"singles out Sabbath observers for special and . . . absolute protection without according similar accommodation to ethical and religious beliefs and
practices of other private employees," should not have resulted in the statute's invalidity.

44. Adams & Emmerich, 137 U. Pa. L. Rev. at 1630–39 ("There is no
evidence, for example, that when the Founders accommodated Quakerism
and other minority sects in the areas of loyalty oaths and conscientious
objection, they believed they were impermissibly 'aiding' religion or 'preferring' such sects over other religions. Indeed, some of the early state constitutions that prohibited governmental preference for one religion over others
also granted loyalty oath and conscientious objector accommodations.");
Mark Tushnet, The Emerging Principle of Accommodation of Religion
(Dubitante), 76 Geo. L.J. 1691, 1699 (1988) (accommodation principle "fits,
albeit not entirely comfortably, into the complex and somewhat inconsistent
structure of government and political theory that the framers had in mind").

mine when the similarly situated criterion is met. Some examples of government's according benefits to one religion that are not meaningfully distinguishable from those withheld from another faith are quite clear: if a city were to have a public display of symbols in recognition of Christmas but not Chanukah, or if the legislature were to grant a sacramental use exemption for wine but not peyote, or if a school board were to permit a religious excuse from attendance at classes in evolution but not sex education, this should be held invalid absent some compelling justification.[45] This is the test the Court uses for deliberate discrimination among religious groups.[46] At the other extreme, an exemption from jury service but not from attendance at certain public school classes plainly does not abridge the equal treatment precept (although the latter failure to excuse may violate the burdensome effect principle). There will certainly be some closer cases, but I believe they will be neither so frequent nor so difficult as to be beyond the Court's reasoned and dispassionate judgment.

Definition of Religion

This chapter's consideration of how to define religion under the intentional advantage principle concerned the question of which types of ideologies, if they were the beneficiaries of deliberate government advantage, would fall within the principle's strictures. Although this broad issue was left unresolved,[47] it is appropriate here to address the narrower question of which kinds of beliefs must be included within an exercise of the government's power of accommodation.

The burdensome effect principle provides a constitutionally *compelled* accommodation only for those religious beliefs that entail extratemporal consequences. But the intentional advantage principle *permits* accommodations for *all* religious beliefs as long as the accommodations do not meaningfully

45. This "strict scrutiny" approach, as we have seen, is almost always "fatal in fact."
46. See chapter 2, notes 5 and 6 above.
47. See pp. 103–8 above.

threaten religious liberty, with the further qualification that the legislative authorization may not treat similarly situated religions differently. How should "religious" beliefs be defined under the intentional advantage principle's mandate of equality? Although it may be acceptable for the Court to adopt any one of several generous definitions of religion[48] to serve this nondiscrimination guarantee, I believe that the category should be governed by the speech, association, *and* religion provisions of the First Amendment and thus include all those "narrow partisan ideologies" that have been made subject to the potential disabilities of the intentional advantage principle to begin with.[49] If this were the approach, I doubt there would be many instances in which a sincerely held ideological belief that would not qualify under one of the inclusive definitions of religion mentioned above would nonetheless become eligible for a voluntarily granted exemption for some religion from a general welfare regulation. But there would probably be some. For example, if a state, assuming it was not constitutionally required to do so, wished to grant a religious exemption from its rule of mandatory school attendance until age sixteen, I would urge that it must also excuse persons like Henry David Thoreau, whose strongly held philosophic views (which might not be considered "religious" even under the embracing definitions mentioned above) called for rejection of contemporary social values and isolation at Walden Pond. A less inclusive rule would permit the majority-influenced political process to favor religious over nonreligious ideologies without any constitutionally imposed strictures—an undesirable position in my judgment.[50]

48. See discussion at pp. 67–86 above.
49. See pp. 103–8 above.
50. I would urge a similarly expansive treatment for the special immunity accorded to "religion" in United States v. Ballard, discussed at p. 91 above, where the Court held that the Free Exercise Clause forbade judicial determinations of whether religious beliefs are "true." Although the verity of beliefs concerning whether supernatural events have taken place—which was at issue in the criminal prosecution for obtaining money under false pretenses in *Ballard*—is especially susceptible to rejection by judges and

It must be conceded that this may well impose substantial obligations on various government agencies, not simply in respect to enhancing the number of groups that would have to be exempted from a general regulation, but also in regard to funding various public programs (especially in the areas of education and artistic expression). On balance this is justified, I think, because fulfillment of the equality element will not likely interfere with the state's ordinary authority to act for the welfare of its people as greatly as will the burdensome effect principle's compelled religious accommodations. Rather, the advantage need only have "a broader impact,"[51] providing government favors to ideologies on a nonpartisan basis. And even were this nondiscrimination requirement to cause the lawmaking body to decide against assisting *any* set of beliefs, that would only prevent government from exercising authority that I believe is relatively marginal in terms of its legitimate function, at least in comparison to its more usual "police power" role.

ENDANGERING RELIGIOUS LIBERTY

The intentional advantage principle permits government accommodations for both mainstream and minority religions, but not if they are achieved at the expense of religious freedom. On the one hand, some people will object because only a meaningful threat to religious liberty will bar the state from

---

juries, I believe that the category of claims that should be free from adjudicative scrutiny should be enlarged to encompass other assertions that are similarly not verifiable through ordinary experience—including all those grounded in some "transcendental" explanation (see pp. 81–83 above), and probably others that we often uncritically speak of as being subject to "scientific proof" (see pp. 83–85 above). Although existing constitutional doctrine has never directly addressed this kind of problem, the Free Speech Clause has been interpreted to advance different policies by placing definite constraints on the state's ability to penalize or award civil damages for the making of false statements. New York Times Co. v. Sullivan, 376 U.S. 255 (1964). The Court would probably impose similar constitutional limits on an allegedly deceived political contributor's damages action against a successful candidate for failing to abide by campaign promises.

51. Railway Express Agency v. New York, 336 U.S. 106, 112 (1949) (Jackson, J., concurring).

deliberately favoring religious interests (especially in the mainstream), even when this may reasonably be perceived as approval or endorsement of religion and may produce legitimate feelings of alienation and offense in a segment of the population.[52] As exemplified by permitting some Christmas and Chanukah displays on public property, this will be seen by separationists as too deferential to the political/religious majority. On the other hand, although (as we shall see) the intentional advantage principle allows imposition of some social costs in order to accommodate religious interests by granting exemptions from state rules that conflict with sincerely held religious tenets, it forbids government's favoring individuals because of their religious beliefs if the benefits have the effect of (a) coercing or significantly influencing people either to violate their existing religious tenets, or to engage in religious activities or adopt religious beliefs when they would not otherwise do so,[53] or (b) compelling people to afford financial support either to their own religion or to that of others.[54] As illustrated by forbidding exemptions from religiously onerous requirements of public benefits programs, this will be opposed by liberals as being inadequately sensitive to the needs of minority religions. And as typified by disapproving government subsidies for chaplains in the military and tax exemptions for church property,[55] it will be

52. See pp. 29–34 above.

53. Similar to the process I have suggested for identifying the "reasonable (or objective) observer" under the endorsement approach (see pp. 28–29 above), the Court's inquiry for determining these issues should be empirically based but ultimately normative, centering on the reaction of an "average" or "reasonable" person in the relevant segment of the population. Since in most instances the surrounding circumstances would be essentially similar throughout the country, the Court should ordinarily apply a nationwide standard. But if it is shown that special sensitivities exist in a particular community, I urge that those factors should govern the question whether there is a meaningful threat to religious liberty. This matter will be referred to several times in the rest of this chapter. For specific illustrations, see notes 134 and 159 below.

54. I have described these forbidden effects elsewhere as "coercing, compromising, or influencing religious beliefs." 41 U. Pitt. L. Rev. at 675. See also 47 Minn. L. Rev. at 330.

55. See pp. 123, 172 below.

resisted by accommodationists (on behalf of mainstream religions) as assigning too activist a role to the judiciary. The rest of this chapter will undertake a fuller justification, explanation, and illustration of the intentional advantage principle's middle-ground position.

ACCOMMODATIONS FOR RELIGIOUS MINORITIES

Whether it is fair to characterize laws that help mainstream religions as constituting merely "accommodations" has already been considered.[56] Here the question is whether government action to facilitate the free exercise of minority religions—regulations that most people would agree are accommodations—should properly be termed lawmaking that *favors* or *benefits* religion and thus fall within the potential invalidity of the intentional advantage principle. Various attempts to define these legislative accommodations as something other than action undertaken for religious purposes have now been generally discredited as "contrived":[57] "To call the purpose 'secular' is to obscure the reality that the purpose to accommodate religion is often not very different from the purpose to promote religion."[58] Other efforts have implicitly (or explicitly) conceded that government facilitations of free exercise favor religion but conclude by "definitional fiat"[59] that they are constitutionally permissible.[60]

A highly persuasive approach for the position that state accommodations of minority religious exercise do not prefer

56. See pp. 98–103 above.
57. Steven D. Smith, Separation and the "Secular": Reconstructing the Disestablishment Decision, 67 Tex. L. Rev. 955, 991 (1989).
58. Kent Greenawalt, Religion as a Concept in Constitutional Law, 72 Calif. L. Rev. 753, 797 (1984).
59. Hall, 65 Temp. L. Rev. at 67.
60. See, e.g., Simson, The Establishment Clause in the Supreme Court: Rethinking the Court's Approach, 72 Corn. L. Rev. 905, 913 (1987); Mark Tushnet, Reflections on the Role of Purpose in the Jurisprudence of the Religion Clauses, 27 Wm. & Mary L. Rev. 997, 1007–8 (1986); John N. Moore, The Supreme Court and the Relationship between the "Establishment" and "Free Exercise" Clauses, 42 Tex. L. Rev. 142, 196–97 (1963); Choper, 47 Minn. L. Rev. at 395–96 n. 436.

or favor these religions was initially developed by Marc Galanter. He contended that exemptions for small religions from general government regulations amount to no more than equalizing the position of these minorities with that of the majority. He was the first to base his thesis on the now commonly accepted premise[61] that "[w]hatever seriously interferes with majority religious beliefs and practices is unlikely to become a legal requirement—for example, work on Sunday or Christmas."[62] In direct support of his argument, he pointed to the leading Free Exercise Clause decision of *Sherbert v. Verner*.[63] In that case a millworker who was a Seventh-Day Adventist was discharged by her employer when she would not work on Saturday, the Sabbath day of her faith, after all the mills in her area adopted a six-day workweek. South Carolina denied her unemployment compensation benefits for refusing to accept "suitable work," even though that would require her to work on Saturday. The Court held that this violated the Free Exercise Clause because "to condition the availability of benefits upon [her] willingness to violate a cardinal principle of her religious faith effectively penalizes the free exercise of her constitutional liberties."[64] Although the Court did not materially rely on it, the unemployment compensation statute involved in *Sherbert* prohibited any disadvantage against employees who refused to work on Sunday because of their religion and thereby "expressly save[d] the Sunday worshipper from having to make the kind of choice"[65] imposed on Sherbert. Thus, Galanter reasoned, special treatment for religious minorities is restorative or equalizing, ordinarily granting them only "what majorities have by virtue of suffrage and representative government."[66]

61. See p. 57 above.
62. Marc S. Galanter, Religious Freedoms in the United States: A Turning Point? 1966 Wis. L. Rev. 217, 291.
63. 374 U.S. 398 (1963).
64. Id. at 406.
65. Id.
66. Galanter, 1966 Wis. L. Rev. at 291.

TAX-FINANCED SUBSIDY OF RELIGION

This approach has several deficiencies of differing degrees of significance. The first, of only peripheral import, is that it assumes the validity of certain advantages that mainstream religions may create for themselves. But if what the majority obtains "by virtue of suffrage" itself contravenes the restrictions of the intentional advantage principle, then providing the same benefit to religious minorities compounds the violation rather than eliminating it. Thus the devotional Bible reading and Lord's Prayer programs struck down by the Court (correctly, in my view, as we shall see) could not have been cured by reading from the Torah, the Koran, and works of secular philosophy on selected days of the month. In the *Sherbert* case, since those who refused to work on Saturdays for nonreligious reasons, such as watching football games or spending the day with their children, would not obtain unemployment benefits under South Carolina's scheme (and could constitutionally be denied them under the Court's ruling), it seems clear that when Sherbert is excused from taking otherwise suitable work because of her religious scruples, the purpose of the exemption is solely to facilitate her religious exercise. Moreover, the exemption meaningfully impairs religious liberty in one of the most historically objectionable forms, because compulsorily raised tax funds would be used to subsidize Sherbert's exercise of religion. Thus it runs afoul of the intentional advantage principle.[67] Similarly, since the exemption for Sunday worshipers granted by South Carolina, as much as the exemption for Sherbert mandated by the Supreme Court, favored religion and involved religious coercion in the form of a tax subsidy for religious practice, it too would violate the Establishment Clause under my thesis.[68]

67. This being so, it plainly follows that no exemption is required under the burdensome effect principle.

68. It is true that most Christians will also enjoy the more general advantage of the Gregorian calendar, which makes it much more likely that mills will operate on Saturday than on Sunday, and that Sunday worshipers

Second, and more fundamental, I believe that the core values of the Religion Clauses should not be overlooked when government seeks to alleviate burdens imposed on religious minorities by generally applicable regulations. If "restoring" the minority to a position of "equality" with mainstream religious sects results in impairment of religious liberty, it is forbidden by the intentional advantage principle. Sherbert's right to freely exercise her religion does not encompass government assistance that infringes the religious freedom of other citizens by forcing them to subsidize her religious practice. The Religion Clauses should bar government from implementing one person's religious liberty at the expense of another's.

The strength of this analysis is not weakened, I contend, by the fact that the government aid does not result in what Alan Schwarz's important article described as the "imposition of religion"[69] by "inducing religious choice"[70] (*actually influencing* a person's beliefs), rather than merely helping to "implement a religious or irreligious choice independently made."[71] This approach would apparently not invalidate a tax subsidy of religion unless it met that criterion. But as we have seen, the framers considered taxation in support of churches to be an especially reprehensible form of religious coercion, a view maintained within the contemporary value of protecting religious freedom. Under the "no imposition" approach, many such subsidies would seemingly be permissi-

---

therefore will usually not be confronted with the choice Sherbert faced. But as we have seen analogously, pp. 46–48 above, that actions currently serving secular purposes happen to have religious roots does not destroy their contemporary neutrality. See, e.g., McGowan v. Maryland, 366 U.S. 420, 444, 451–52 (1961) (modern Sunday closing laws "are of a secular rather than of a religious character"; "it is common knowledge that the first day of the week has come to have special significance as a rest day in this country. . . . The cause is irrelevant; the fact exists").

69. Alan Schwarz, No Imposition of Religion: The Establishment Clause Value, 77 Yale L.J. 692 (1968).

70. This is a phrase used by Chief Justice Rehnquist in a dissenting opinion that, in part, closely followed Schwarz's approach. Thomas v. Review Board, 450 U.S. 707, 727 (1981).

71. Schwarz, 77 Yale L.J. at 728.

ble, even allowing a modest (non-"inducing") public reward for regular attendance at the church of one's choice. These would plainly be forbidden by the intentional advantage principle, even those that might fairly be characterized as restorative or equalizing. For example, although members of a particular sect might demonstrate that they had inadequate funds to buy vestments, largely because of the costs of complying with a state health code's mandate to remove hazardous materials from the church building, it appears beyond dispute that the Establishment Clause should bar a state subsidy for the purchase. If a zoning ordinance, enacted to serve substantial public goals, excluded churches within many miles of particular indigent persons' homes, it is plain that the historical and contemporary command of the Religion Clauses to avoid taxation in aid of religion should prevent the state's funding their weekly transportation to services. Similarly, the intentional advantage principle would proscribe the government's paying chaplains to minister to the religious needs of prisoners and military personnel. It may be that, under the burdensome effect principle, the state could not exclude chaplains who volunteer for these purposes. But under my thesis, the Establishment Clause makes it the financial responsibility of the church and not the state to attend to its members' religious needs. The no imposition approach would enable the state to finance many private religious activities—as opposed to government activities such as prayers in public schools, which undoubtedly influence religious belief[72]—free of Establishment Clause constraints. The intentional advantage principle prevents this.

INDIRECT ECONOMIC AND SOCIAL COSTS

Restorative or equalizing accommodations for religion that do *not* meaningfully interfere with religious freedom should be permissible, however, even though such accommodations may impose substantial costs of certain other kinds on those who are not their beneficiaries. It must be recog-

72. See pp. 140–45 below.

nized that all exemptions from general government regulations exact *some* social or economic tolls, certain of which are
more clearly financial (or monetary) than others. First, as
examples of costs whose pecuniary implications are relatively
remote or nonexistent: relieving a student whose faith bars
formal schooling beyond the eighth grade from the state's
compulsory education law undermines the strong public interest in an informed citizenry; granting a draft exemption
to a religious objector probably means that a nonbeliever who
would otherwise avoid being drafted will be required to serve;
excusing a religious child from the school requirement that
she wear shorts in gym class deprives her classmates of the
desired total uniformity of dress; excepting houses of worship
from a low-density land-use regulation produces many of the
evils of congestion. Similarly, excising evolutionary theory
from public school curricula in order to avoid offending devout believers in a religious theory of creation deprives the
other children of meaningful knowledge.

A second category involves economic costs that are somewhat closer to the tax-financed subsidy in *Sherbert:* for example, if a state granted a Sabbatarian exemption from a Sunday
closing law, other merchants might well object on the ground
that the religious exemption caused them financial injury because, being forced to close on Sundays, they lost business to
their Sabbatarian competitors.

Finally, there are some situations where the costs are
"specifically exacted to facilitate religious interests that the
cost-bearers have no stake in"[73] and thus appear to be little
different from the use of compulsorily raised tax funds in
Sherbert. For example, in *Estate of Thornton v. Caldor, Inc.,*[74] a
state law forbade private employers from demanding that
believers work on their designated Sabbath. Assuming that
this would involve some cost that the employer would either
absorb from profits or pass on to customers, it seems fair to
analogize this coercive regulation of the employer's economic

73. Hall, 65 Temp. L. Rev. at 87.
74. 472 U.S. 703 (1985).

affairs to a tax on some people to support the religious practice of others,[75] or to a public subsidy to the employer "to
defray the additional costs it had to bear to keep the religious
worker on its payroll."[76]

The intentional advantage principle's middle-ground position, which permits religious accommodations as long as
they do not meaningfully threaten religious liberty, requires
that a distinction be drawn at some point between *Sherbert* at
one extreme and, say, the gym class dress code at the other.
This is not done easily, however, because as the foregoing
discussion shows, the fact patterns tend to fall along a spectrum of cost measurement rather than into clearly divided
segments.

One method would be to invoke our historical aversion
to religious assessments and compulsory church contributions and draw the line at direct subsidies: a specific amount
from public tax coffers to religious persons or groups is so
similar to past evils, both economically and analytically, as to
fall plainly within the proscribed class. "The economic cost
and the religious benefit of a direct tax and subsidy are one
and the same; the taxpayer pays the tax and the church receives it."[77] This would invalidate the payment in *Sherbert*
(and other welfare benefit cases to be considered shortly)[78]
but none of the other regulations set forth above.

It appears to be only a short step to also encompass costs
that are clearly measurable and identifiable, albeit only indirectly imposed. This might well bring the Sunday closing law
exemption and *Caldor* regulation within its reach—although
neither the non-Sabbatarian merchant nor the *Caldor* employer (or employees) might be able to prove meaningful
financial loss. But even apart from the ambiguity contained

75. Lupu, 140 U. Pa. L. Rev. at 593.

76. Richard A. Epstein, Religious Liberty in the Welfare State, 31 Wm.
& Mary L. Rev. 375, 406 (1990).

77. Michael W. McConnell, Accommodation of Religion, 1985 Sup.
Ct. Rev. 1, 38–39.

78. Based on the discussion at pp. 18–19 above, this reasoning would
apply to tax exemptions as well.

in the term "costs that are clearly measurable and identifiable," there is strong reason for preferring the *direct* subsidy test. Unlike the tax payment in *Sherbert,* the indirect economic and social costs are not required to satisfy the believer's needs. The Sabbatarian store owner who seeks to remain open on Sunday does not demand that the non-Sabbatarian be closed on that day so that the Sabbatarian may acquire the non-Sabbatarian's customers; they are an unsought benefit, and the Sabbatarian's free exercise claim could be fully satisfied without them. Nor does the religious pacifist need to have another do military service in his place; the price imposed on the nonbelieving draftee does not aid the exempted person's religious beliefs at all. Nor is it necessary to the religious tenets of the fundamentalist that nonbelieving children fail to learn about Darwin. In contrast, Sherbert claimed a constitutional right to have tax funds subsidize the observance of her Sabbath. The pocketbook injury to nonbelieving taxpayers was necessary to accomplish this religious end. The cost itself served to benefit religion rather than resulting incidentally from the accommodation of religious exercise. If accommodations for religion impose this kind of religious charge on nonbelievers, then they are forbidden by the intentional advantage principle. But in conformance with the reality that securing individual constitutional rights often (or almost always) imposes impediments to the smooth functioning of our system, if accommodations for religion impose only imprecise social/economic costs, then these prices of religious tolerance are permitted to be paid.

ILLUSTRATIONS OF RELIGIOUS EXEMPTIONS

The burdensome effect principle addresses the question of when religious exceptions from general government rules are required by the Free Exercise Clause, while the intentional advantage principle concerns the matter of when these special benefits are permitted by the Establishment Clause. This section explores the prohibition of both principles against exemptions that meaningfully threaten religious freedom: it applies the thesis to a range of fact patterns as well as to important Supreme Court decisions on the subject (other than *Sherbert* and *Caldor*, which have just been discussed at some length).

First, there is a group of cases in which it appears highly unlikely that a religious exemption would meaningfully endanger religious liberty (as that term has been explained above). In *Yoder*,[79] since there seems to be no real possibility that relieving students from the state's requirement of school attendance until age sixteen would in some way significantly influence others to accept the Amish faith in order to obtain this benefit, the exemption could not be successfully challenged under the Establishment Clause. Other situations that lend themselves to the same analysis, because it is extremely doubtful that credible proof would be forthcoming that people would be influenced to adopt religious beliefs that they would not otherwise hold, include *Quaring v. Peterson*,[80] in which the Court affirmed a ruling that the Free Exercise Clause demanded an exemption from the state's requirement of photographs on all driver's licenses for a person whose religious belief was that having her picture taken violated the Second Commandment's bar on "graven images"; *Goldman v. Weinberger*,[81] holding that the Free Exercise Clause did not require the air force to exempt from its dress code an Orthodox Jewish psychologist who wished to wear a yarmulke while on duty in uniform at a military hospital; and the criminal prohibition addressed in the peyote case,[82] where it appeared that few persons desire to ingest peyote for nonreligious purposes, probably because of its nausea- and depression-inducing quality[83] and the availability of alternative recre-

---

79. 406 U.S. 205 (1972).

80. 728 F.2d 1121 (8th Cir. 1984), aff'd by an equally divided Court, 472 U.S. 478 (1985).

81. 475 U.S. 503 (1986).

82. Discussed at length in chapter 2.

83. "The consensus among the peyotists with whom I have worked . . . is that taking peyote is hard: the taste is bitter, the nausea unpleasant, the anxiety and depression overwhelming, and the night's ritual performance

ational drugs without this side effect. Similarly, "if the government exempts Sikh construction workers from the safety requirement of wearing a hard hat (which conflicts with their religion), this exemption will not make it more desirable for individuals to adopt the Sikh religion. . . . Allowing Jewish prisoners a special diet will not encourage kosher eating (as long as the alternative meals are no better than the standard fare); allowing Amish buggy drivers not to display a bright orange triangle will not induce conversions to the Amish religion."[84] Nor could it be seriously argued that exempting children with religious objections from having to wear shorts in gym class would cause other pupils to consider changing their religion so that they too might be excused.

The draft exemption cases fall into a second category. The Court has never held that the Free Exercise Clause requires release for those who object to military service on religious grounds. Indeed, at a time close to the high-water mark of its solicitude for religious liberty, the Court held in *Gillette v. United States*[85] that the Free Exercise Clause does not require excusing those whose faith prohibits participation only in particular wars (rather than in all wars) and strongly suggested that "relief for conscientious objectors is not *mandated* by the Constitution."[86] But may Congress *voluntarily grant* such an immunity without abridging the intentional advantage principle?

We have already observed that religious excuses from conscription impose substantial costs on nonbelieving draftees who must take the religious objectors' place, but that these

---

taxing." David F. Aberle, The Peyote Religion among the Navajo 9 (1966). It also has been observed, however, that for some users peyote produces "a warm and pleasant euphoria, an agreeable point of view, relaxation, colorful visual distortions, and a sense of timelessness." Omer C. Stewart, Peyote Religion: A History 3 (1987). Still, there has been no evidence presented that the exemption for sacramental use granted by the federal government and many states, see note 39 above, has attracted converts to the Native American Church.

84. McConnell, 60 Geo. Wash. L. Rev. at 701.

85. 401 U.S. 437 (1971).

86. Id. at 461 n. 23 (emphasis added).

"imprecise social/economic" costs are not themselves enough to condemn the exemption under the Establishment Clause. Nonetheless, they do serve as a warning signal that the advantage for religion may be so great as to impermissibly induce nonbelievers to profess religious belief and ultimately undergo genuine conversion. This would be contrary to the intentional advantage principle, as well as being inconsistent with James Madison's general approval of state accommodations for religion. "While he supported constitutional exemptions for religious individuals from laws that would compel them to violate their 'religious[] scrup[les],' he opposed measures that would convey upon persons of certain religious faiths 'extraordinary privileges, by which proselytes may be enticed from all others.'"[87]

The Selective Service Law of 1917, which exempted from combat duty only those religious objectors who belonged to "well-recognized" religious sects,[88] posed some danger of truly influencing people to adopt particular religions.[89] The more broadly worded exemption in effect during the Vietnam War era—applying to any person "who, by reason of religious training and belief, is conscientiously opposed to participation in war in any form"[90]—was significantly less likely to induce people to join established churches either from sincere conviction or simply for the sake of convenience. In addition, the Court's expansive reading of that provision[91]—making it available "if an individual . . . holds beliefs that are purely ethical or moral in source and content but . . . nevertheless impose upon him a duty of conscience to refrain from participating in any war at any time"[92]—reduced that risk even further. Still, professing a personal "religion" (as opposed to "essentially political, sociological, or philosophical

87. McConnell, 60 Geo. Wash. L. Rev. at 700 (quoting Madison).
88. Selective Service Law of 1917, chap. 15, § 4, 40 stat. 78 (1917).
89. This provision would, in any event, violate the intentional advantage principle's equality requirement that accommodations not treat "similarly situated" religious practices differently.
90. 50 U.S.C. § 456(j) (1976).
91. See pp. 67–69 above.
92. Welsh v. United States, 398 U.S. 333, 340 (1970).

considerations")[93] was enough to gain the enormous advantage of avoiding battle and therefore would likely tempt bona fide religious choice. Indeed, since the government was authorized to examine the sincerity of an objector's religious beliefs,[94] it seems that at least some claimants might be prompted to join established churches to corroborate their positions.[95] Even if not, potential draftees seeking exemption would have to formulate a statement of personal doctrine that would pass muster. This endeavor would involve deep and careful thought and perhaps reading in philosophy and religion. Some undoubtedly would be persuaded by what they studied. Indeed, it seems likely that the strong temptation to adopt a religion might well produce a sincere belief without any underlying bad faith. Moreover, the theory of "cognitive dissonance"[96]—which posits that to avoid madness we tend to become what we hold ourselves to be and what others believe us to be—also suggests that some initially fraudulent claims of belief in a personal religion (which do not amount to violations of religious tenets or unfeigned acceptance of a new faith) would ripen into true adherence.

93. United States v. Seeger, 380 U.S. 163, 165 (1965).

94. See p. 91 above.

95. It is obviously impossible to gather precise information on the number of fraudulent applications for conscientious objector status, or on the number of such claims that ripened into true belief. It is interesting to note, however, that a number of handbooks published during the Vietnam War era recommended tactics for asserting questionable claims. One manual, for example, suggested that "many who consider themselves to be 'selective objectors' find that they can qualify for CO status by taking what might be called an existential approach." CCCO, Handbook for Conscientious Objectors 4 (12th ed. 1972). It is also interesting that the percentage of registrants classified as conscientious objectors increased sharply in the late 1960s, a time of widespread political opposition to military service. See [1973] U.S. Dir. Selective Serv. Semi-Ann. Rep., July 1–Dec. 31, at 32.

96. See generally Robert A. Wicklund & Jack W. Brehm, Perspectives on Cognitive Dissonance (1976); Russell H. Fazio et al., Dissonance and Self-Perception: An Integrative View of Each Theory's Proper Domain of Application, 13 J. Exper. Soc. Psych. 464 (1977); Leon Festinger, Conflict, Decision, and Dissonance (1964); Leon Festinger, A Theory of Cognitive Dissonance (1957); Leon Festinger & James M. Carlsmith, Cognitive Consequences of Forced Compliance, 58 J. Abnorm. & Soc. Psych. 203 (Mar. 1959).

Thus a draft exemption for religious objectors seriously threatens values of religious freedom by encouraging the assumption of religious beliefs by those who seek to qualify for the benefit. It would be unconstitutional under the intentional advantage principle.

This should be contrasted with the case of non-Sabbatarian merchants who coveted the Sabbatarian exemption from the Sunday closing law because they felt it was more profitable to be open on Sundays than on Saturdays. It is possible that some such persons would be led to misrepresent their religious beliefs to obtain the privilege. But I believe that the intrinsic motivational difference between conscientious opposition to war and the comparatively crass desire for pecuniary gain makes it extremely unlikely that the non-Sabbatarian's actual beliefs would be influenced in the process. Therefore the Establishment Clause should not bar that accommodation for religion.

The third group of decisions, like *Sherbert* but unlike those in the two categories just reviewed, involves government taxes and expenditures. Three cases, all involving tax exemptions, directly parallel *Sherbert* both analytically and economically.[97] In *Texas Monthly, Inc. v. Bullock*,[98] the Court held that a state sales tax exemption limited to religious publications violated the Establishment Clause. Since the law favored religion through compelled financial support, it would fail the test of the intentional advantage principle, as would an immunity from a state sales and use tax for purchasing religious materials that was unsuccessfully sought under the Free Exercise Clause in *Jimmy Swaggart Ministries v. Board of Equalization*.[99] So too would the exception for religious schools from the denial of tax exempt status for engaging in racial discrimination, as was claimed under the Free Exercise Clause in *Bob Jones University v. United States*[100] but refused by the Court. Although other aspects of *Bob Jones University*

97. See discussion of tax exemption, pp. 18–19 above.
98. 489 U.S. 1 (1989).
99. 493 U.S. 378 (1990).
100. 461 U.S. 574 (1983).

may present a persuasive case for inclusion under the burdensome effect principle,[101] the element of subsidy would cause the requested special treatment to violate the Establishment Clause.

A variation is presented by the facts of *Bowen v. Roy*,[102] which raised (but did not explicitly decide)[103] the question whether the Free Exercise Clause mandates a religious exception from the government rule that welfare recipients must obtain a social security number. The case is indistinguishable from *Sherbert* under the intentional advantage principle: the *Roy* exemption would involve a special payment for religion and accordingly violate the Establishment Clause. But if the government wished to accommodate those whose religious tenets make acquisition of a social security number harmful to spiritual development, it could probably still do so by simply assigning a number (as it in fact did in the case before the Court) without requiring that registration actually be applied for.[104]

A final tax exemption case, however, presents facts that appear to survive the bar against compelling citizens to afford

101. See Mayer G. Freed & Daniel D. Polsby, Race, Religion, and Public Policy: Bob Jones University v. United States, 1983 Sup. Ct. Rev. 1, 22–24 & n. 55 (refusal in *Yoder* to defer to government interest in universal compulsory education cannot be reconciled with recognition in *Bob Jones* of a compelling government interest in eliminating racial discrimination in education); Douglas Laycock, Tax Exemptions for Racially Discriminatory Religious Schools, 60 Tex. L. Rev. 259, 275 (1982) (national policy of fostering racial equality involved in *Bob Jones* "too attenuated to justify interference" with internal affairs of pervasively religious schools unless religious schools "so take over the public function of educating white students that desegregated education outside those church schools becomes impossible").

102. 476 U.S. 693 (1986).

103. See Choper, 70 Neb. L. Rev. at 657 n. 36, and chapter 3, note 139 above.

104. Despite the appearance of a government funded preference for religion, this procedure does not grant a true exemption from the overall purposes of the government program. In contrast to *Sherbert*, where the state was ordered to subsidize religion despite the fact that its goal of requiring "suitable work" was unfulfilled, here the government's interest in all welfare recipients' having social security numbers would be satisfied at no real cost.

financial support to religion. In *United States v. Lee*,[105] an Amish farmer unsuccessfully sought a Free Exercise Clause exemption from paying social security taxes on the wages of his Amish employees on the ground that the Amish believed it was sinful not to provide for financially dependent members of their community.[106] At first glance the case seems to be squarely covered by the earlier analysis of *Sherbert, Texas Monthly, Jimmy Swaggart Ministries,* and *Bob Jones University.* But the Amish tenet involved in *Lee* forbade not only contribution of social security taxes, but also receipt of social security assistance. If it were true, as Justice Stevens persuasively contended in his separate concurrence, that an exemption for Amish employers "probably would benefit the social security system because the nonpayment of these taxes by the Amish would be more than offset by the elimination of their right to collect benefits,"[107] then the social security system would suffer no net diminution in revenue, there would be no public subsidy of religion, and an exemption would be permissible.

CONSENT EXCEPTION

A major qualification of the "no coercing or significantly influencing religious beliefs" precept[108] remains to be explored. In *Corporation of the Presiding Bishop of the Church of Jesus Christ of Latter-Day Saints v. Amos*,[109] a building engineer in a gymnasium owned by the Mormon Church was fired because he failed to maintain membership in good standing in the church. The Court held that the statutory exemption for religious institutions from the prohibition of Title VII of the Civil Rights Act of 1964[110] against religious discrimina-

---

105. 455 U.S. 252 (1982).

106. For criticism of the Court's ruling in view of its then existing doctrine, see Choper, 70 Neb. L. Rev. at 663–65.

107. 455 U.S. at 262 (Stevens, J., concurring).

108. See p. 118 above.

109. 483 U.S. 327 (1987).

110. 42 U.S.C. §§ 2000e(j), 2000e-2(a), 2000e-1(a) (Supp. IV 1988).

tion in employment, permitting churches to favor members of their own faith in the workplace, did not violate the Establishment Clause. Like the non-Sabbatarian merchants who desired the Sabbatarian exemption from the Sunday closing law because they felt it was more profitable to be open on Sundays than on Saturdays, it is possible that some non-Mormons would be led to misrepresent their religious faith in order to obtain employment. But it seems unlikely that it could be demonstrated that their true beliefs would be meaningfully affected in the process. On the other hand, it seems quite plausible that a threatened loss of employment might significantly influence some people with previously existing commitments to the church to continue their sincere adherence to the tenets of the religion that are required for good standing even though they would not otherwise wish to do so. Would the congressionally granted exemption from Title VII in favor of religion therefore be invalid under the intentional advantage principle?

There are several possible routes in attempting to reach a negative response. One contention is that it is inaccurate to describe the exemption as favoring religion: "Title VII does not prohibit discrimination on the basis of secular ideology; secular, ideological organizations are permitted to discriminate in favor of their adherents. The Sierra Club can hire only environmentalists if it chooses. Though in form the exemption upheld in *Amos* was religion-specific, in effect it merely placed religious organizations on the same plane as their nonreligious counterparts."[111]

This argument raises a nice issue of what constitutes "discrimination." Viewed from the perspective stated, the point is irrefutable. But from the vantage point of what types of groups may use sectarian criteria in employment, religious organizations are plainly favored: the Mormon Church but not the Sierra Club may discriminate based on creed. As the Court acknowledged, the provision "singles out religious enti-

111. McConnell, 60 Geo. Wash. L. Rev. at 731 n. 209.

ties for a benefit,"[112] and as the author of the contention under review himself conceded, the law "explicitly exempt[s] only religious organizations from its scope."[113] The government authorized church groups to act in a way that impaired the free religious choice of their members. This appears to be unconstitutional under the intentional advantage principle.

Second, it may be forcefully urged that it is inaccurate to describe the exemption as government's enabling churches to impair the religious freedom of their members. Viewed from one perspective, Title VII and the exemption for religious organizations do no more than restore the prelegislative status quo. Before the Civil Rights Act was passed, it was not unlawful for church groups to discriminate based on religion. This is precisely the legal status of such conduct at present. Indeed, given the powerful dictates of faith that cause some churches to favor their own members in the work of the church (in contrast to other religions that might aggressively reject religious discrimination in employment), there is no strong reason to believe that the two-step legislative maneuver has meaningfully encouraged any additional discrimination.[114]

This argument raises in turn a nice issue of what constitutes "state action."[115] Although the contention's theoretical thrust has real force,[116] it also contains genuine difficulties. The broadest objection is that the "maintenance of the status quo" *always* results when an exemption is made from a rule, and it seems not to make any significant analytic difference whether the special immunity was granted contemporaneously with or subsequent to enactment of the general regulation. Moreover, although it is generally conceded that gov-

112. 483 U.S. at 338.

113. McConnell, 60 Geo. Wash. L. Rev. at 696.

114. For a fair argument to the contrary, see Tushnet, 76 Geo. L.J. at 1710–11.

115. See generally Tushnet, 76 Geo. L.J. 1691.

116. See Jesse H. Choper, Thoughts on State Action: The "Government Function" and "Power Theory" Approaches, 1979 Wash. U. L.Q. 757, 762.

ernment *repeal* of an existing prohibition ordinarily ends the state's constitutional responsibility for subsequent private conduct,[117] the *Amos* situation is not the same as a repeal. Rather, it is more accurate to describe an exemption as a partial (or selective) repeal, specifically favoring those who are its beneficiaries. The exemption from Title VII is an act of government that singles out religious organizations for special privileges, and it creates a meaningful danger to the free choice of employee-members of the church. That this threat to religious liberty depends on the action of a nongovernment agent (the church) should no more affect the relevance of the intentional advantage principle than the fact that, as we shall see shortly, peer group pressure from fellow students is requisite for the compromise of religious beliefs connected with "voluntary" prayer and Bible reading programs in public schools. Nonetheless, the Court has never held that a legislature is generally barred from granting a racially/religiously selective repeal of a right that the lawmakers had previously created, that is, a right not guaranteed by the Constitution as an original matter. Indeed, as I have discussed elsewhere,[118] it is an exceedingly complex question whether the state should be constitutionally responsible in this context for the conduct of individuals that had once been permitted, was forbidden by law, but is now tolerated because of the prohibition's repeal.

Fortunately there is a more promising line of reasoning for permitting government, within the intentional advantage principle, to authorize churches to meaningfully influence the free religious choice of their members, or for allowing the Court, within the burdensome effect principle, to hold that the Free Exercise Clause requires that churches have this special power in some circumstances. The dispensation rests

117. See Crawford v. Los Angeles Board of Education, 458 U.S. 527 (1982).

118. See Jesse H. Choper, The Repeal of Remedies for De Facto School Segregation, in Jesse H. Choper, Yale Kamisar, & Laurence H. Tribe, The Supreme Court: Trends and Developments, 1981–82 49–53 (1983).

in the idea of "consent": a church's members agree to abide by its rules in respect to matters of faith and thus waive their right to object. Several of the Supreme Court's earliest and most important decisions on the Religion Clauses clearly establish this precept: "The right to organize voluntary religious associations . . . and to create tribunals for the decision of controverted questions of faith . . . is unquestioned. All who unite themselves to such a body do so with an implied consent to this government, and are bound to submit to it."[119] The basis for the Court's edict has been helpfully articulated by Michael McConnell: "The premise of the Religion Clauses is that individuals are capable of choice in the religious realm and the government is not.[120] And if believers choose to subordinate their material interests to the religious body, the government . . . [need not] protect the individual from the consequences of his religious convictions. To be sure, this may mean that the church will adopt policies that seem to the outsider unjust, unwise, or exploitative. For better or worse, the church may not always conform to the outside world. But it is of no concern of the government to reform the church. The government's legitimate interest extends no further than the material sphere."[121]

Consent (or choice, or waiver) is, however, a complex concept.[122] Ordinarily, voluntariness is a key ingredient. According to the precept of consent being discussed here, "peo-

---

119. Serbian Eastern Orthodox Diocese v. Milivojevich, 426 U.S. 696, 711–12 (1976), quoting Watson v. Jones, 80 U.S. (13 Wall.) 679, 728–29 (1872). See also Gonzalez v. Archbishop of Manila, 280 U.S. 1, 16 (1929); Presbyterian Church v. Hull Church, 393 U.S. 440, 446–47 (1969). For historical support of this view, see Michael W. McConnell, Free Exercise Revisionism and the Smith Decision, 57 U. Chi. L. Rev. 1109, 1145 (1990).

120. The concept of "choice" in this context is merely a secular interpretation of the religious experience. In some traditions the believer is understood to have been chosen, rather than as having done the choosing. (Footnote in original.)

121. Michael W. McConnell, Neutrality under the Religion Clauses, 81 Nw. U. L. Rev. 146, 159 (1986). (I have slightly amended McConnell's point.)

122. See Edward L. Rubin, Toward a General Theory of Waiver, 28 UCLA L. Rev. 478 (1981).

ple get together and organize churches by a kind of corporate contract. Membership is voluntary. New members consent to the rules when they contract in. And the parties can rewrite the contract at any time before a dispute arises,"[123] but of course *not thereafter* (at least not unilaterally).

In some situations, however, it may be too glib to say that "membership is voluntary." What about those who have belonged to a church since birth? It may be that their initial affiliation was not "voluntary," but their continuing to be members as adults is surely consensual. But what about social or economic pressures that may keep people on board—for example, spouses or grown children arguing that they adhered in order to maintain family harmony, or the building engineer in *Amos* contending that he persevered as a Mormon in order to keep his job? Although each of these points has merit, none seems persuasive enough, in my judgment, to overcome the essential contractual nature of persons becoming and remaining members of a church. The dynamic of consent and the concomitant reliance of other congregants permits government to side with religious groups against their members in respect to matters of faith without undermining the intentional advantage principle.[124]

123. John H. Garvey, Churches and the Free Exercise of Religion, 4 Notre Dame J.L. Eth. & Pub. Pol'y 567, 572 (1990).

124. A number of commentators have invoked this idea of consent, with varying degrees of emphasis, as a justification for resolving the conflict they find respecting (1) the Free Exercise Clause rights of the individual congregant and (2) the similarly secured constitutional rights of the other members of the faith as individuals; and (3) the religious freedom of the members banded together collectively and (4) the church's First Amendment right to religious autonomy. In this weighing of liberalism's concern for the individual and civic republicanism's attention to community (see generally Michael J. Sandel, Freedom of Conscience or Freedom of Choice? in Articles of Faith, Articles of Peace: The Religious Liberty Clauses and the American Public Philosophy 74 [James D. Hunter & Os Guinness eds., 1990]), the balance is struck in favor of restrictions on the religious liberty of some persons in this context as being necessary for the greater overall religious liberty to flourish. See generally Frederick M. Gedicks, Toward a Constitutional Jurisprudence of Religious Group Rights, 1989 Wis. L. Rev. 99; Ira M. Ellman, Driven from the Tribunal: Judicial Resolution of Internal Church Disputes, 69 Calif. L. Rev. 1378 (1981); Douglas Laycock, Towards a General Theory of the Religion Clauses: The Case of Church Labor

A final issue concerns the scope of the members' consent to the law of their church. It has been generally described to this point as their concurrence with rules "in respect to matters of faith." More specifically, it should include all tenets that the religious organization and its members sincerely believe to be "necessary for the [religious] community's self-definition,"[125] with one important exception: as was true under the burdensome effect principle, the state should be able to regulate the relationship between congregants and their churches, even when consensual, if the state has a sufficient interest in doing so. The level of scrutiny that the Court applies should depend on whether a constitutional freedom is being burdened, a right established either under the Religion

Relations and the Right to Church Autonomy, 81 Colum. L. Rev. 1373 (1981); Garvey, 4 Notre Dame J.L. Eth. & Pub. Pol'y 567; McConnell, 81 Nw. U. L. Rev. 146 (1986); Gerard V. Bradley, Commentary on West & Garvey, 4 Notre Dame J.L. Eth. & Pub. Pol'y 639 (1990).

My point is slightly different, although not inconsistent. Rather than disposing of the member's constitutional right under the Religion Clauses because it is outweighed by the free exercise rights of others, I conclude that the member waives the right otherwise protected under the intentional advantage and burdensome effect principles.

The logical extension of this use of the consent/choice/waiver precept in regard to a church's relationship with its own members also encompasses my thesis as to judicial resolution of internal religious disputes, which largely tracks the Court's present approach. Just as members should be held to agree to their church's rules on matters of faith, they ought also to be treated as implicitly consenting to the proposition that, absent an understanding to the contrary, "civil courts are bound to accept the decisions of the highest judicatories of a religious organization of hierarchical polity on matters of discipline, faith, internal organization, or ecclesiastical rule, custom or law . . . whether or not rational or measurable by objective criteria," Serbian Orthodox Diocese v. Milivojevich, 426 U.S. 696, 713–15 (1976). Members of congregational churches similarly should be bound to agree that "authority over questions of church doctrine, practice, and administration rests entirely in the local congregation or some body within it." Jones v. Wolf, 443 U.S. 595, 619 (1979) (Powell, J., dissenting). In accord with the earlier discussion of the issue of using government power to promote "nonreligious" ideology, pp. 103–8 above, I believe there is much to be said for interpreting the First Amendment freedom of association guarantee to mandate an analogous rule of judicial deference for all intraorganizational disputes involving the ideological tenets of the group.

125. Corporation of the Presiding Bishop v. Amos, 483 U.S. 327, 343 (1987) (Brennan, J., concurring).

Clauses pursuant to the thesis of this book or under some other constitutional provision.

RELIGION IN THE PUBLIC SCHOOLS

Religious practices and influences in the public schools have been among the most frequently litigated issues, and probably *the* most controversial constitutional subject, in the church/state area. As already discussed,[126] it is beyond fair dispute that government programs of vocal and silent prayer, Bible reading, invocations by clergy at graduation, excising the teaching of evolution, and posting religious symbols in classrooms all favor religious interests. So too do laws that require courses in creation science, as will be discussed later in this chapter. To these should be added "released time"—a system under which pupils whose parents express a desire for them to have religious instruction are excused from regular classes for a specified period each week, while children who do not participate in the religious teaching given during this time remain for secular courses or study halls. All these practices come within the coverage of the intentional advantage principle, and their validity therefore should turn on whether they pose a meaningful threat to religious liberty.

PEER GROUP PRESSURE

Some situations are easily decided. If a public school were to require all students to recite a prayer, or to bow their heads (or even to stand silently and respectfully) while others prayed, this formally compelled participation in the religious exercise would plainly be unconstitutional. But most of the public school religious programs of this kind that have come to the Supreme Court—prayer and Bible reading, released time for religious instruction, graduation invocations—have been voluntary: objecting students were excused from being present. Nonetheless, in all such cases but one (*Zorach v.*

126. See pp. 50–52 above.

Clauson,[127] involving released time for religion classes conducted off the premises of the school), the Court found a violation of the Establishment Clause. Apart from *Zorach,* these results comport with the intentional advantage principle because of the almost universally accepted idea that young people of minority religious groups are extremely sensitive about conspicuously absenting themselves from religious activities conducted by the majority: there is a powerful, albeit subtle, pressure to conform. The emotional strain is frequently so great that it results in unwilling participation in preference to some degree of social ostracism.

Social psychologists and sociologists have pointed out that children place great importance on how they are esteemed by their peers. The urge to conform to their classmates' attitudes is peculiarly potent,[128] and "the fear of being accused by the others of wanting to be 'different'" and the "very strong need to remain a member of one's group"[129] are carried so far as to cause these children to do and say things in accordance with the majority that they are convinced are wrong, even with reference to simple perceptual materials.[130] This is particularly prevalent "where the situation is ambiguous."[131] The option either to participate in the majority's religious worship or "to suffer the pain of psychic loneliness"[132] forces these immature students "to choose between equally

127. 343 U.S. 306 (1952).

128. See Clay V. Brittain, Adolescent Choices and Parent-Peer Cross-Pressures, 28 Am. Sociol. Rev. 385 (June 1963); Donna R. Clasen & B. Bradford Brown, The Multidimensionality of Peer Pressure in Adolescence, 14 J. Youth & Adolescence 451 (Dec. 1985); B. Bradford Brown, Donna R. Clasen, & Sue A. Eicher, Perceptions of Peer Pressure, Peer Conformity Dispositions, and Self-Reported Behavior among Adolescents, 22 Develop. Psychol. 521 (July 1986). The insight is not new. See Gardner Murphy & Lois B. Murphy, Experimental Social Psychology 511–16 (1931).

129. Ruth W. Berenda, The Influence of the Group on the Judgments of Children 30 (1950).

130. Id. at 16–33.

131. Id. at 32.

132. Address by Professor Robert Bierstedt, The Use of Public Schools for Religious Purposes, ACLU Biennial Conference, June 22, 1962, p. 10. Bierstedt was then chair of the Department of Sociology and Anthropology at the New York University Graduate School of Arts and Sciences.

intolerable alternatives."[133] Indeed, many religious educators warn "that so-called voluntary exemption [from religious observances] does not overcome the compulsion exerted by majority behavior."[134] Thus, in my view, the inclusion of the words "under God" in the Pledge of Allegiance to the American flag—a phrase added, according to the House Report on the amendment, to affirm the dependence of "our people and our Government upon the moral directions of the Creator"[135]—is probably unconstitutional.[136]

That these public school religious practices are inherently

133. Id.

134. Committee on Religion and Public Education of the National Council of the Churches of Christ, Relation of Religion to Public Education—A Study Document, Int. J. Relig. Ed., April 1960, pp. 21, 29. See also John C. Murray, Law or Prepossessions? 14 Law & Contemp. Prob. 23, 39 (1949): "Thousands of educators of all religious convictions are increasingly agreed that the atmosphere of public schools is *not* free from pressures."

Elsewhere I have detailed specific evidence that, because they inherently involve coercion, vocal prayer, Bible reading, and released time for religious instruction (whether on or off premises) meaningfully threaten religious liberty and should be held unconstitutional. 47 Minn. L. Rev. at 368–400. As for invocation prayers at graduation, although I once briefly speculated that the situation may not endanger religious freedom, id. at 408, I have been persuaded to the contrary by Justice Kennedy's opinion for the Court in Lee v. Weisman, 112 S.Ct. 2649 (1992), stressing that "in our culture high school graduation is one of life's most significant occasions," id. at 2659, where "the school district's supervision and control," id. at 2658, place "subtle coercive pressures," id. at 2656, "on attending students to stand as a group or, at least, maintain respectful silence during the Invocation and Benediction." Id. at 2658.

135. H.R. Rep. no. 1693, 83 Cong., 2d sess. 2 (1954).

136. For fuller consideration of this "difficult question," see Choper, 47 Minn. L. Rev. at 410–11. An "even closer question" is presented by the school exercise of singing patriotic songs that involve supplications to the deity, such as "God Bless America," "America the Beautiful," the third stanza of "The Star-Spangled Banner," and the last stanza of "America." As to whether these may be immunized under the intentional advantage principle because their thrust is not to favor or benefit religion, see id. at 411. For discussion of the celebration in the public schools of certain holidays of mainstream religions by using symbols (compare Easter bunnies and Christmas trees with crucifixes and menorahs), or by singing religious songs (compare "Jingle Bells" and "White Christmas" with "Silent Night"), or by staging religious pageants (compare Dickens's "Christmas Carol" with a play depicting the birth of Christ), see id. at 411–13.

compulsive may be demonstrated by examining the factual situations in some of the litigated cases. Terry McCollum, whose mother, an ardent atheist, successfully challenged a program of released time religion classes on public school premises in Champaign, Illinois,[137] exercised his right of non-participation only during the first semester of fourth grade; the next semester he attended religion classes. The following year he changed schools. In the first semester of fifth grade, he and only one other pupil declined to attend religion classes; during the second semester, the other boy capitulated.[138] In Terry's new school "children of some thirty-one sects, including Catholic, Jewish, and Protestant, as well as many children without any particular religious preference,"[139] *voluntarily* attended a course teaching the tenets of Protestantism. Donna Schempp's father, who was of the Unitarian faith, effectively challenged Bible reading in the Abington Township, Pennsylvania, public schools as being contrary to his family's religious beliefs.[140] Donna had never voiced her objections to school authorities and on occasion had even volunteered to read the Bible herself.[141] Although New York provided that any child could leave the room during recitation of the Regents' Prayer, none had requested permission to do so.[142] In southern elementary schools there were established periods of Christian Bible study; Jewish children had the option of leaving the room, but "some believe[d] that it [was] better to remain seated than to have forty-three children watch one or two others shuffle out."[143]

More generally, over the years, schools with released time

137. See McCollum v. Board of Education, 333 U.S. 203 (1948).

138. See McCollum v. Board of Education, 396 Ill. 14, 17, 71 N.E.2d 161, 162 (1947).

139. Record, p. 65, McCollum v. Board of Education, 333 U.S. 203 (1948).

140. Schempp v. School District, 177 F. Supp. 398 (E.D. Pa. 1959).

141. Id. at 400.

142. Brief for Petitioners, p. 31, Engel v. Vitale, 370 U.S. 421 (1962).

143. Harry L. Golden, quoted in Leo Pfeffer, Church, State and Freedom 304 (1953). "The Christian children wonder why one or two of their number 'do not want to hear about God,' and the Jewish child is also heartsick as well as bewildered." Id.

programs have reported "a considerable percentage of pupils in attendance whose parents do not belong to any church."[144] "They want to go to the church with their schoolmates and ask their parents to sign release cards."[145] Where released time systems have been abandoned, attendance at religion classes has declined.[146] Children of minority religious faiths have been known to enroll in the majority's religion classes because they did "not wish to be marked."[147] Those who chose not to enroll, or who were forbidden by their parents to do so, have told of being "ostracized by the other children in after-school activities."[148]

It is probably inevitable in our society that adherents of small sects and nonbelievers will be subjected to some scorn and derision. Because of this, societal pressures will be

144. Jerome C. Jackson & Constantine F. Malmberg, Religious Education and the State 39 (1928).

145. Russell N. Sullivan, Religious Education in the Schools, 14 Law & Contemp. Prob. 92, 94 (1949).

146. See id. at 111.

147. Leo Pfeffer & Phil Baum, Public School Sectarianism and the Jewish Child: A Report of Experiences 19 (1957). See Record, p. 135, McCollum v. Board of Education, 333 U.S. 203 (1948), in which Terry McCollum's teacher testified that she spoke to Terry's mother about "the fact that allowing him to take the religious education course might help him to become a member of the group. He was not accepted as a member of our class. I thought if he did the same things that they were doing that might help."

148. Affidavit quoted in Leo Pfeffer, Church, State, and Freedom 357 (1953). "When the released time students departed . . . I felt left behind. The released children made remarks about my being Jewish and I was made very much aware of the fact that I did not participate with them in the released time program. I endured a great deal of anguish as a result of this and decided that I would like to go along with the other children to the church center rather than continue to expose myself to such harassment. I asked my mother for permission to participate in the released time program and to accompany my Catholic classmates to their religious center, but she forbade it." Id. at 356; accord, id. at 356–67. Contra, Gertrude B. Corcoran, Social Relationships of Elementary School Children and the Released-Time Religious Education Program (unpublished doctoral dissertation in Stanford University Library), abstracted in 56 Relig. Ed. 363–64 (1961), concluding that the "degree of participation in the released-time program was not demonstrably related to the sociometric status of elementary school children."

brought to bear on members of religious minorities to forsake their beliefs. As long as these societal pressures are initiated by "private action," the Constitution affords no self-executing relief. But the intentional advantage principle does not permit a government program that is undertaken to favor religion to increase the price of being a religious nonconformist.

NONCOERCIVE PROGRAMS

The cases involving evolution, creation science, silent prayer, and posting the Ten Commandments are factually distinguishable from the practices just considered because the former programs included no formal provision for excusal from participation. But just as the "voluntary" aspect did not save prayer and released time, neither does the "mandatory" element of these other endeavors necessarily invalidate them. Indeed, although the argument is not conclusive in respect to all of these practices, I believe that none significantly threatens religious liberty. Thus, contrary to the Supreme Court's decisions in all four cases, they are not unconstitutional under the intentional advantage principle.

In *Epperson v. Arksansas*,[149] the Court held that an "anti-evolution" statute, which made it unlawful to teach the theory of Charles Darwin in the public schools, violated the Religion Clauses. The Court rested its conclusion on the ground that it was "clear that fundamentalist sectarian conviction was and is the law's reason for existence."[150] I would not dispute the Court's finding that the statute intentionally favored religion. But to invalidate a religiously motivated law that creates none of the dangers the Religion Clauses were designed to prevent represents, in my view, an "untutored devotion to the concept of neutrality"[151] between church and state. Conceding that the law in *Epperson* benefited fundamentalist religions, there was no evidence that religious beliefs were coerced or significantly influenced. That is, it was not shown, nor do I believe

149. 393 U.S. 97 (1968).
150. Id. at 107–8.
151. Abington School District v. Schempp, 374 U.S. 203, 306 (1963) (Goldberg, J., concurring).

it could be persuasively argued, that the anti-evolution law either induced children of fundamentalist religions to accept the biblical theory of creation or conditioned other students for conversion to fundamentalism. In contrast to the other situations discussed above, those youngsters whose religious interests were not advanced by the law appeared to suffer no harm to their religious liberty. Thus the accommodation for the religious needs of the majority should have been upheld.

In *Edwards v. Aguillard*,[152] the Court ruled that a Louisiana statute requiring the teaching of "creation science" in the public schools whenever evolution was taught violated the Establishment Clause. The Court concluded that the law's purpose was to "endorse a particular religious doctrine."[153] The dissenters' contention, that the legislature had sought to "protec[t] academic freedom" by expanding the number of scientific theories to be taught respecting the origin of the species[154] may have been accurate as to some lawmakers. Still, I would find that the statute's purpose was to benefit religion. As in *Epperson,* the law's overwhelming (if not exclusive) impetus was to placate those religious fundamentalists whose beliefs reject the Darwinian theory of evolution.[155] But as long as the theory of creation science is taught in a noncommittal (or objective) rather than a dogmatic (or proselytizing) fashion, it does not seem to pose a danger to religious liberty. Indeed, if based on "a fair and balanced presentation of the scientific evidence,"[156] such a course would add to the well-rounded education of students. Taught in that fashion, it would be no more constitutionally vulnerable under the intentional advantage principle than a public school program

152. 482 U.S. 578 (1987).

153. Id. at 594.

154. Id. at 627 (Scalia, J., dissenting).

155. "They are independent thinkers who insist on a right to their own means for seeking knowledge of the world, and they deny the right of the state to tell their children that their worldview is wrong." Stephen L. Carter, Evolutionism, Creationism, and Treating Religion as a Hobby, 1987 Duke L.J. 977, 981.

156. 482 U.S. at 627 (Scalia, J., dissenting).

that sought to prevent children from growing up as religious illiterates by ensuring that they comprehend the role religion has played in this country's evolution and have some understanding of the nature of the conscientious beliefs most of our citizens possess. Similarly, there should be (and is) no constitutional objection to an academic program in comparative religion or to the study of the Bible as an artistic work.[157] The salient distinction is that this would be teaching objectively *about* religion and the Bible and would not be religious indoctrination.

In *Stone v. Graham*,[158] the Court found violative of the Establishment Clause a Kentucky statute requiring that a copy of the Ten Commandments, paid for by private funds, be posted in every public school classroom. I agree with the Court's conclusion that the law's intent was to favor religion, but since the program was funded by private contributions, there was no use of taxes to support a sectarian cause. Moreover, I am not persuaded that anyone's religious beliefs are coerced or influenced in any significant way by simply having this religious message posted in the classrooms.[159]

In *Wallace v. Jaffree*,[160] the Court held that an Alabama statute, requiring a minute of silence for "meditation or voluntary prayer" at the beginning of every public school day,

157. See note 13 above.
158. 449 U.S. 39 (1980).
159. That there may be reasonable disagreement with this judgment—which is ultimately grounded in both empirical and normative inquiries that my thesis unavoidably (but unapologetically) cedes to the judiciary, see note 53 above—is demonstrated by the fact that my intuitive appraisal of the pertinent dynamics caused me to reach the opposite conclusion three decades ago. 47 Minn. L. Rev. at 408–9 ("identification of the public schools with these religiously oriented mottoes, constantly in view of immature students with malleable minds and highest regard for the public school institution, is likely to result in influencing or compromising their religious beliefs"). See also note 134 above. Of course, if any of the underlying factual premises advanced here in respect to these public school practices were found by the courts to be incorrect, the results suggested would have to be changed.
160. 472 U.S. 38 (1985).

violated the Establishment Clause. Again I concur in the Court's finding that the law was passed for one reason only: "to return prayer to the public schools."[161] (Indeed, at least within current vision, I believe this is the purpose of all moment of silence statutes.) But since I do not believe that a minute of quiet for prayer poses any meaningful danger to religious liberty, there would be no violation of the Establishment Clause under the intentional advantage principle.

There is a critical difference between an opportunity for silent prayer in the schools and a program of vocal prayer or Bible reading. In the latter instances, as we have seen, even if children are given the opportunity to be excused, they are going to feel peer pressure to participate. But there is nothing in a moment of silence situation that is going to make any pupil feel coerced to engage in any religious experience. Those who want to pray may do so. Those who are atheists can contemplate why there is no God. Others can simply meditate. Since no students can really know the subject of their classmates' reflections, none will in any way be compelled to alter their thoughts. In my experience the greater likelihood is that during the period of silence many, if not most, elementary and secondary school children will turn their attention to matters having nothing to do with religion.[162]

161. Id. at 59.

162. It may be persuasively argued that the Court should adopt a prophylactic rule on the ground that the program is inherently subject to abuse by teachers, a number of whom will subtly (or not so subtly) urge students to pray (or to act in some other spiritual way). See Arnold H. Loewy, Rethinking Government Neutrality towards Religion under the Establishment Clause: The Untapped Potential of Justice O'Connor's Insight, 64 N.C. L. Rev. 1049, 1068 (1986). In support of this position, it may be contended that the task of policing this constitutionally impermissible conduct in the multitude of public school classrooms across the nation is so vast as to exceed judicial capacity. But judicial action of this kind must depend on the strength of the factual case that is made for it. See, for example, the extensive documentation of the experience over the years with released time that revealed teachers' persistent application of direct pressures on pupils to attend religious classes, even though they had been specifically prohibited from doing so. Pfeffer, Church, State, and Freedom at 356–67; Note, 61 Yale L.J. 405, 412–13 (1952).

RANGE OF ALTERNATIVES

The final decision to be considered regarding religion in the public schools is *Board of Education v. Mergens*,[163] which involved the Equal Access Act: Congress prohibited public secondary schools that received federal funds and that maintained a "limited open forum"—which exists whenever a school permits "noncurriculum related student groups to meet on school premises during noninstructional time"[164]— from denying "equal access" based on the content of the speech at such meetings. The Court held that a school's permitting a Christian students' club to meet for the purpose "among other things . . . to read and discuss the Bible, to have fellowship, and to pray together"[165] did not violate the Establishment Clause. The case presents questions under both parts of the intentional advantage principle: whether the Equal Access Act "favors" religion, and whether it poses a "meaningful threat to religious liberty."

We have already explored, in several related contexts,[166] the consequences of including religious groups within a broader category receiving government benefits; the topic will be further discussed in chapter 5 in respect to public financial aid. Here the question under the intentional advantage principle is whether the state's selecting religious groups as one of a number of beneficiaries may be said to "favor religious interests or benefit individuals because of their religious beliefs." Although the conclusion is by no means indisputable, it seems to me that as long as the process of inclusion and exclusion requires government to pass judgment on the group's purposes or activities, even under very broadly stated criteria,[167] when the state accords its imprimatur it may fairly be viewed as "favoring" (or "benefiting") the chosen group.

By this reasoning, the Equal Access Act is subject to the intentional advantage principle. Nonetheless, it does not con-

163. 496 U.S. 226 (1990).
164. Id. at 235.
165. Id. at 232.
166. See pp. 22–23, 32–33 above.
167. See p. 32 above.

travene the Establishment Clause because it poses no meaningful threat to religious liberty. First, there appears to be no significant disbursement of state funds or use of public resources. Further, as Justice Kennedy noted, the act "does not authorize school authorities to require, or even to encourage, students to become members of a religious club or to attend a club's meetings, . . . the meetings take place while school is not in session, . . . and the Act does not compel any school employee to participate in, or to attend, a club's meetings or activities."[168] Moreover, the record disclosed that "students may choose from approximately 30 recognized groups on a voluntary basis,"[169] including band, chess club, cheerleaders, choir, speech and debate, future business leaders of America, international club, Latin club, math club, and dramatics. This "broad spectrum of officially recognized student clubs"[170] presented a wide range of attractive alternatives to the Christian club and, accordingly, eliminated any peer group coercion to participate in its religious activities.

The same approach applies in a number of analogous situations. The clearest is a program of "dismissed time," "the system under which, on one or more days, the public school closes earlier [or opens later] than usual, and all children are dismissed, with the expectation—but not the requirement—that some will use the dismissed period for participation in religious instruction."[171] It is certainly fair to conclude that since the school board's purpose in early closing was to encourage greater attendance at religion classes than would otherwise occur,[172] this was government action that deliberately favored religious interests. Nevertheless, the element of state-generated compulsion is absent. Students are not faced with the publicly imposed choice of either going to religious school or remaining behind in an unenticing setting. If they choose

168. 496 U.S. at 261 (opinion of Kennedy, J.).
169. Id. at 231.
170. Id. at 252.
171. Pfeffer, Church, State and Freedom at 315.
172. See Wilber G. Katz, Freedom of Religion and State Neutrality, 20 U. Chi. L. Rev. 426, 439 (1953).

to attend religion classes, they will do so in preference to other equally alluring, and in many cases more than similarly attractive, alternatives.[173] Perhaps some children will nonetheless be subject to pressures from their conforming colleagues who choose to attend religion classes,[174] but this would exist even if the schools closed (or opened) at the regular hour. Unlike the case of released time, the coercion may not be attributed to government action.

A similar analysis would validate a variant of the on-premises released time program properly rejected by the Court in *McCollum v. Board of Education.*[175] Under the traditional system of released time, the only alternative to remaining in regular public school courses or study halls is to attend religion classes. This is not the case with a plan that would permit students to be released for a certain period of time each week on condition that they attend one of a group of extracurricular education courses—for example, classes in music, art, religion, or drama.[176] Providing desirable activities as an alternative to religious education would remove the inherently coercive element in conventional released time. Students who either were religious nonconformists or had marginal beliefs would not be faced with the choice of either receiving religious instruction, which would compromise or influence their conscientious scruples, or being regarded as "oddballs." They could join those of their friends of the religious majority who preferred to study art, music, or drama rather than religion. It may be that if such a program were instituted more children would attend religion classes than would otherwise do so, and that this was the school board's

173. "[R]eligion can compete more successfully with arithmetic than with recreation." Note, 57 Yale L.J. 1114, 1119 (1948).

174. See generally 31 Tex. L. Rev. 327 (1953).

175. 333 U.S. 203 (1948).

176. "Released time as now practiced had its origin in Gary, Indiana, in 1913 when the then Superintendent of Schools directed the dismissal of children an hour earlier one day of each week to enable them to pursue their individual interests such as religion, music or art." Leo Pfeffer, Religion, Education and the Constitution, 8 Law. Guild Rev. 387, 396–97 (1948).

intent. But even though this would involve government action to favor religion by making it easier to follow religious pursuits, the absence of coercion calls for a favorable constitutional judgment under the intentional advantage principle. State action of this nature may fairly be characterized as merely an "accommodation."

Public schools have traditionally granted excused absences to students for observance of their particular religious holidays. This is plainly a benefit to religion under the intentional advantage principle. Further, it carries the potential of influencing the excused students to attend services at the church or synagogue of their choice because of peer group pressures imposed by their coreligionists. If the schools were to condition the permitted absence on the students' participation in religious services, there should be a clear violation of the Establishment Clause. But if there is a general excusal opportunity for all pupils of a particular religion on their holiday, the similarity to the Equal Access Act in *Mergens,* to dismissed time, and to "released time with a range of extracurricular choices" appears to acquit the practice.

The situation in *Widmar v. Vincent*[177] completes our discussion of this topic. The Court held that the Establishment Clause did not bar a public university, which permitted all student groups to use a public forum for meetings and activities, from allowing its use by a religious group that wanted it "for religious worship and religious discussion."[178] As in *Mergens,* the university's authorization favored religion. But the practice passes muster under the intentional advantage principle because although there may have been some measurable imputed rental value for use of the premises, there was no meaningful expenditure of tax funds or other cost to the public for religious ends and no other significant danger to religious freedom.[179]

177. 454 U.S. 263 (1981).
178. Id. at 265.
179. The Court's recent decision in Lamb's Chapel v. Center Moriches Union Free School District, 113 S.Ct. 2141 (1993), involving the use of

OFFICIAL ACKNOWLEDGMENT OF RELIGION

Although "there is an unbroken history of official acknowledgment by all three branches of government of the role of religion in American life from at least 1789,"[180] it was not until the mid-1980s that the Court actually resolved a specific challenge to one of these practices. A review of these prominent examples of government action undertaken to accommodate mainstream religions rounds out our exploration of the intentional advantage principle.

PRAYERS BY GOVERNMENT OFFICERS

In *Marsh v. Chambers,*[181] the Court upheld Nebraska's paying a chaplain $320 per month to begin each day that the legislature was in session with a prayer. The opinion relied on history, on long-standing tradition at both the federal and state levels, and on the specific intent of the framers.[182] Since it is plain that this policy deliberately favored religion, and since there was a meaningful expenditure of tax-raised funds, thus abridging religious liberty, the case would be decided differently under the intentional advantage principle. This should be contrasted with a judge's daily practice of reciting a prayer immediately on being seated after opening court.[183] Although this favors religious interests no differently than does the legislative prayer, it *may* be distinguishable from *Marsh:* it clearly involves no meaningful expenditure of tax funds and, unlike prayer ceremonies in public school classrooms or at graduation exercises, it may not impose even subtle pressures on mature adults present in the courtroom to stand in silence or to signify participation in any other way.

---

public school property during nonschool hours for presentation of a religious perspective on family matters when other views were permitted, was properly held to be governed by *Widmar.*

180. Lynch, 465 U.S. at 674.

181. 463 U.S. 783 (1983).

182. Id. at 786–92.

183. See North Carolina Civil Liberties Union Legal Foundation v. Constangy, 947 F.2d 1145 (4th Cir. 1991) (Establishment Clause violation).

DISPLAYS ON PUBLIC PROPERTY

The other Supreme Court decisions in this area have involved exhibits recognizing Christmas and Chanukah. In *Lynch v. Donnelly*,[184] each holiday season the city of Pawtucket, Rhode Island, in cooperation with a merchants' group, placed a large Christmas display in a privately owned park: a Santa Claus house, reindeer pulling Santa's sleigh, a Christmas tree, carolers, and a "Season's Greetings" banner, as well as a nativity scene depicting the birth of Christ. The total cost of the crèche, paid for ten years earlier, was $1,365, an expenditure not challenged in the litigation. It currently cost the city about $20 annually to erect and dismantle the display. There was no maintenance expense over the ten-year period. The Court held that inclusion of the nativity scene in this otherwise secularly oriented Christmas display did not violate the Establishment Clause.

This ruling comports with the intentional advantage principle. Despite the Court's heroic efforts to find "legitimate secular purposes,"[185] inclusion of the nativity scene must fairly be described as government action that favored religion.[186] And there is no disputing that the crèche offended strict separationists. But there does not appear to be any significant danger to religious liberty. No one was compelled or meaningfully influenced to do anything in respect to their religious beliefs, and to the extent that tax funds were used at present, the amount seems to have been de minimis. Although it may well be that, as a matter of policy, public agencies should avoid the dissension and discomfort engendered by displaying symbols with such strong sectarian overtones, the Court should not hold them to be unconstitutional.

This reasoning extends to the "two recurring holiday displays located on public property in downtown Pittsburgh" at issue in *Allegheny County v. ACLU*,[187] in which the Court up-

---

184. 465 U.S. 668 (1984).
185. 465 U.S. at 681.
186. See p. 99 above.
187. 492 U.S. 573, 578 (1989).

held the placement just outside the city-county building of a Chanukah menorah (owned by a Jewish religious group) next to a Christmas tree and a sign saluting liberty, but invalidated the location of a crèche (owned by a Catholic religious group) on the grand staircase of the county courthouse. Both displays would be permissible under the intentional advantage principle, as would a city's endorsing a private civic group's use of a public park to mount "their annual yuletide display of sixteen large paintings depicting various events in the life of Jesus Christ"[188] and a village's including, as part of its annual Italian cultural festival held in a public park, a Catholic mass (recited in Italian) in a tent that would be used at other times during the day as a beer garden and concert hall.[189] In contrast, a city's spending "more than $200,000 to construct a special platform and to provide other extraordinary assistance" for the celebration of a mass by Pope John Paul II[190] would run afoul of the intentional advantage principle's bar against significant expenditures of tax funds to deliberately benefit religion.

PAID VACATION ON GOOD FRIDAY

Several appellate court decisions challenging a state's making Good Friday a paid holiday for public employees provide a helpful additional illustration of both parts of the intentional advantage principle. First, although the matter is not uncomplicated,[191] when it is stripped to the core it seems clear that because Good Friday is a "day of solemn religious observance,"[192] the state's action deliberately favors religious interests by placing the state's "imprimatur on both the Christian rites and practices observed on that day and to Western

188. Doe v. Small, 934 F.2d 743, 746 (7th Cir. 1991) (Establishment Clause violation).
189. Doe v. Village of Crestwood, 917 F.2d 1476 (7th Cir. 1990) (Establishment Clause violation).
190. Gilfillan v. City of Philadelphia, 637 F.2d 924 (3d Cir. 1980) (Establishment Clause violation).
191. See Cammack v. Waihee, 932 F.2d 765, 773–77 (9th Cir. 1991).
192. Haw. H. Stand. Comm. Rep. no. 254 (H. Bill no. 39), quoted in 932 F.2d at 775.

Christianity in general."[193] Unlike Sunday, Christmas, and Thanksgiving, "Good Friday is associated with the religious symbol of Jesus Christ on the cross . . . [and is] bereft of secular symbols or joyous festivity."[194] Even the court that refused to adhere to the implications of this conclusion nonetheless declined to "accept the contention that the observation of 'Good Friday' in the Western Christian world has become 'secularized' in the same manner as Thanksgiving and Christmas celebrations have become in this country."[195]

But agreeing that the state's rule was intended to benefit religion is only the first step toward invalidation under the Establishment Clause. A meaningful interference with religious freedom is also required. There would be no disputing such a finding if it were clear that the state expenditure was being made only to support the observance of the holiday. That was the case when California closed all state offices on Good Friday between noon and 3:00 P.M., the traditional time for worship, and paid its workers.[196] But if state employees were entitled to a designated number of paid holidays and Good Friday was simply chosen for a spring respite because it was a day "on which many people choose to be absent from work for religious reasons,"[197] then it would be fair to characterize this as a *costless* way for the state to "accommodate the widespread religious practices of its citizenry."[198] This was the essence of the Court's reasoning in *McGowan v. Maryland*,[199] upholding the state's choosing Sunday as "an appropriate choice for a weekly uniform day of rest because the community to a large degree already so regarded Sunday, due to its religious significance and (no doubt) to the long tradition of Sunday Closing Laws."[200]

193. 932 F.2d at 788 (dissenting opinion).
194. Id. at 790.
195. Id. at 782 n. 19.
196. Mandel v. Hodges, 54 Cal. App.3d 596, 127 Cal. Rptr. 244 (1976) (unconstitutional).
197. Cammack, 932 F.2d at 777.
198. Id.
199. 366 U.S. 420 (1961).
200. Commack, 932 F.2d at 778.

AN EXTREME (AND UNLIKELY) HYPOTHETICAL

Last, it must be conceded that the requisite of a tangible danger to religious freedom may permit some very troublesome hypothetical government actions—much more distressing than a national day of thanksgiving to God, or "In God We Trust" as our national motto, or a Latin cross on a city's seal[201]—to survive a constitutional challenge urging *judicial invalidation.* For example—recognizing that the most disturbing cases are more frequently the products of creative hypotheticals than of the authentic dynamics of government action—if a municipality were to announce that "Christianity is our religion," it would probably not violate the intentional advantage principle if the city did nothing beyond its proclamation; that is, if it did not spend tax funds or require or encourage any sort of action on the part of its citizens.[202] If the city council did engage in this unlikely undertaking, and if the state legislature chose to ignore it, and if the state courts did not find it invalid under the state constitution, and if Congress took no action, then I would be willing to accept the fact that the *Supreme Court would not strike it down under the Religion Clauses* even though the municipality's action seems to serve no beneficial end and unmistakably represents the specter of a specific evil that the Establishment Clause seeks to prevent.[203]

Of course I am aware of the strong likelihood that if such a highly improbable situation actually arose, the Court would find a way to conclude, under some provision of the Constitution, that this *explicit adoption of a single, official faith* was invalid. But I believe that the price of forcing a broad legal principle to reach the "very worst case" (albeit an extremely

201. See text at chapter 1, note 122 above. See also Fox v. City of Los Angeles, 22 Cal.3d 792, 587 P.2d 663, 150 Cal. Rptr. 867 (1978) (display of Latin cross on city hall on Christmas and Easter).

202. Compare Wooley v. Maynard, 430 U.S. 705 (1977) (state motto on automobile license plates).

203. "The only universal element of every establishment was government endorsement of one or more religions." Douglas Laycock, "Noncoercive" Support for Religion: Another False Claim about the Establishment Clause, 26 Val. U. L. Rev. 37, 42 (1991).

implausible one) is often unacceptably high when weighed against the virtues of the norm's application to ordinary and recurring circumstances. As Frank Easterbrook put it, "the parade of horribles is nothing but an argument against rules and serves (if indulged) to undermine rather than strengthen the claim for judicial review."[204] Thus, although the "endorsement" approach would satisfy our historically grounded concerns and basic contemporary intuitions about this fictitious municipal proclamation, we have earlier seen that, when fairly applied to a range of contexts, it would be unduly restrictive of government's ability to accommodate both mainstream and minority religions. The cost of such a "perfect" rule in an imperfect world is usually just too great.

A NOTE ON APPLICATION OF THE ESTABLISHMENT CLAUSE TO THE STATES

The Court has long held that the Fourteenth Amendment caused both Religion Clauses to place limits on the states as well as on the federal government,[205] once noting that contrary arguments "seem entirely untenable and of value only as academic exercises."[206] Nonetheless, beginning soon after the initial ruling and continuing to the present time, distinguished scholars have questioned application of the Establishment Clause to the states.[207] The essence of their reasoning has been that, unlike the Free Exercise Clause, the nonestablishment provision forbids enactments that "affect most remotely, if at all, the personal rights of religious lib-

204. Frank H. Easterbrook, Abstraction and Authority, 59 U. Chi. L. Rev. 349, 378 (1992).
205. Cantwell v. Connecticut, 310 U.S. 296 (1940) (Free Exercise Clause); Everson v. Board of Education, 330 U.S. 1 (1947) (Establishment Clause).
206. Schempp, 374 U.S. at 217.
207. See Edward S. Corwin, A Constitution of Powers in a Secular State 111–16 (1951); Mark de W. Howe, The Constitutional Question, in Religion and the Free Society 49 (Fund for the Republic 1958); Paul A. Freund, The Supreme Court of the United States: Its Business, Purposes, and Performance, 58–59 (1961); Akhil Reed Amar, The Bill of Rights as a Constitution, 100 Yale L.J. 1131, 1157–60 (1991).

erty"[208] and therefore cannot logically be absorbed by the relevant Fourteenth Amendment language that "no State shall . . . deprive any person of life, liberty, or property, without due process of law."

"The fallacy in this contention," however, in the words of Justice Brennan, "is that it underestimates the role of the Establishment Clause as a co-guarantor, with the Free Exercise Clause, of religious liberty."[209] In addition, a central feature of my thesis has been that a tangible danger to religious freedom is mandatory for a *judicial ruling* that the Establishment Clause has been abridged. As we have just seen, this precept makes some quite plain constitutional transgressions untouchable under the Religion Clauses through a challenge in the federal courts. But it also readily incorporates violations of the Establishment Clause within the judicial branch's authority to enforce the Fourteenth Amendment, a step explicitly consistent with the latter's applicable language.

208. Howe, The Constitutional Question at 55.
209. Schempp, 374 U.S. at 256 (Brennan, J., concurring).

5

....

Independent Impact Principle

Even if its purpose is nonreligious and it has general applicability, government action that benefits religious interests and has no independent secular impact should be held to violate the Establishment Clause if the action poses a meaningful danger to religious liberty.

The major difference between the state regulations to be considered here and those that were the subject of chapter 4 concerns their intent. If it is determined that government action *deliberately* seeks to provide an advantage to religion *and* that it significantly affects religious freedom, then it violates the intentional advantage principle regardless of whether it has any nonreligious consequences. To recall an earlier illustration:[1] even if the memory skills of first-graders in a predominantly Catholic school district are sharply improved by compulsory learning of the catechism, the program violates the Establishment Clause because of its religious purpose and liberty-threatening effect.

As I have already observed several times, however, many government efforts that almost all people would agree are undertaken to advance the secular public welfare, irrespective of their impact on religious interests, may well be attributable to religious roots and consequently advance religious concerns. For example, legislators who favor a disarmament program because they strongly believe it will promote world peace may well be deeply influenced by pacifist ideals grounded in their early religious training or present faith. Moreover, there are also times when some (or many) mem-

---

1. See chapter 4, note 2 above.

bers of a lawmaking body may act for dual purposes: to achieve an unquestionably legitimate secular goal and, simultaneously, to further religious ends. For example, legislators may vote for a Sunday closing law in order both to encourage church attendance *and* to set aside "a day of rest, repose, recreation . . . a day which all members of the family and community have the opportunity to spend and enjoy together"[2] (or as suggested in the case, to respond to businesses' wish not to incur operating costs for seven days instead of six for the same amount of sales revenue).[3] Or the lawmakers may favor state aid to nonpublic schools both to relieve their churches' financial demands *and* to improve the overall quality of elementary and secondary education. Or they may support the public restoration of church buildings (e.g., Catholic missions) that have historical, architectural, and educational value both to direct public funds to their religions *and* to encourage tourism that will pay financial dividends to the state treasury in excess of the cost.[4] Finally, there are occasions when a law that is enacted to serve public-welfare ends produces a substantial benefit to religion that no (or virtually no) legislators ever contemplated. This occurred with the program in *Witters v. Washington Department of Services for the Blind*,[5] which provided state vocational education assistance to the visually handicapped and was used by one recipient at a Christian college "in order to equip himself for a career as a pastor, missionary or youth director."[6] Of course, there will be many instances in a multimember legislature when some lawmakers will fit into all three of the categories of motivation just described. These three kinds of government action—undertaken for (1) secular purposes, but traceable to religious influences, (2) both secular and religious purposes, and (3) secular purposes, but with inadvertent benefit to religion—arise much more frequently than regulations subject to the

2. McGowan v. Maryland, 366 U.S. 420, 450 (1960).
3. Id. at 435.
4. See Frohliger v. Richardson, 63 Cal. App. 209, 218 P. 497 (1923).
5. 474 U.S. 481 (1986).
6. Id. at 483.

intentional advantage principle. These are the concern of the "independent impact" principle, under which all such laws are valid if they produce what may be called an "independent secular effect."

REASONS FOR VALIDATION

It should take little effort to demonstrate that laws of the type we have been considering should not be held to violate the Establishment Clause simply because they benefit religion. From a practical perspective, we have already observed that judicial invalidation of all enactments grounded in religious values (category 1 above) would mean that the bars against murder and stealing could not survive, to mention only the most obvious of the countless number of desired and desirable public regulations that would be constitutionally infirm. (This analysis would also apply to government action with unintended religious gains—category 3 above.) From the standpoint of judicial administrability, we have also discussed the seeming impossibility of separating religious from worldly influences in the psyches of the legislators. Moreover, as a matter of constitutional values, if the Court were to disallow government regulations that were assignable to religious precepts, this would make "religious idealism . . . less worthy than post-Kantian, post-Hegelian, post-modernist (or any other) idealism."[7] Although, as I have already noted and shall soon develop more fully, there are circumstances in which my thesis calls for religion to be "disfavored"—in which government is forbidden to grant advantages to religious interests that it affords to others that appear to be similarly situated—this should not extend to restricting the kinds of beliefs that are catalysts for lawmaking. Especially when the product of the legislative or administrative process does not meaningfully impair religious liberty, not only should the Establishment Clause permit government officials to be stimulated by ideological values of any kind, but a contrary

7. Gary C. Leedes, Taking the Bible Seriously, 1987 Am. B. Found. Res. J. 311, 312.

rule would abridge the Free Exercise Clause under the deliberate disadvantage principle.[8] Finally, if laws were overturned because their sponsors used religious arguments in support, legislators would be encouraged "to hide their true purposes . . . [and force] underground the very political process that cannot be stopped."[9] Although concealment may be inevitable in connection with any judicial probe of legislative motive, this delicate inquiry should be reserved for the clearest (and most egregious) situations,[10] which usually involve no substantial independent secular impact.

It is less axiomatic that government action that benefits religion in a way that at least a number of the lawmakers intended (category 2 above) and that also threatens religious freedom should not be held to violate the Establishment Clause for those reasons alone. For example, if it is shown that an identifiable group of legislators voted to fund the refurbishing of Catholic missions only because they wanted to help their faith, should this not be unconstitutional? If it is proved that another set of lawmakers supported a Sunday closing law exclusively because they believed it would increase church attendance, should this not be enough to invalidate it, particularly if the state "has other means at its disposal to accomplish its secular purpose . . . [e.g.,] a regulation demanding that everyone rest one day in seven, leaving the choice of the day to the individual"?[11]

Under the independent impact principle, these statutes do not abridge the Religion Clauses as long as they have an independent secular effect. There are situations in which lawmakers obviously set out to use the machinery of govern-

8. "Nor would Madison deny the right of religious groups as such to petition the government, to support or oppose government policies or candidates for public office, or even actively to campaign." Paul J. Weber, James Madison and Religious Equality: The Perfect Separation, 44 Rev. Pol. 163, 185 (1992).

9. Michael D. Lieder, Religious Pluralism and Education in Historical Perspective: A Critique of the Supreme Court's Establishment Clause Jurisprudence, 22 Wake Forest L. Rev. 813, 883 (1987).

10. See pp. 44–48 above.

11. McGowan, 366 U.S. at 449–50.

ment for the benefit of religion; sometimes they offer plainly implausible nonreligious explanations to defend these enactments.[12] Under the intentional advantage principle the Court, guided by good judgment as confirmed by general societal perceptions, should reject these transparent efforts to rationalize the government's action. But there is a vast difference—one of so great a degree as to approach being a difference in kind—between these sorts of laws and those for which multiple motivations are truly at play. In these latter instances, the judicial task of discerning what prompted a majority (or plurality) of the legislators to act is both too difficult and too intrusive: it might even require the Court to review the fire department's decision to fight a blaze at a local church.

More important, if the legislators' efforts have achieved a legitimate secular goal of real substance, in contrast to one that may be found to have "a mere rational relationship to some valid nonreligious purpose"[13]—and, under my hypothesis, the former alternative is precisely what many lawmakers intended to produce—then I believe that the values of the Establishment Clause have been satisfied. When society receives a public good, that this happens to harmonize with the tenets of some or all religions (as do laws against homicide and theft), or that some or all faiths simultaneously benefit, is simply the reality of a government system that broadly regulates worldly matters. If the Christian Brothers Winery presents the low bid on a contract to supply wine to a state agency, the public's interest in getting the best value for its money is in no way diluted—nor should the Establishment Clause be violated—because a religious group concomitantly reaps a substantial profit. The analysis is not altered because the Christian Brothers' financial gain may be spent exclusively to spread their faith, thus resulting in public funds being used to advance a sectarian ideology. The state's secular objective (acquisition of a product at a good price) has been

12. See pp. 50–52 above.
13. See pp. 52–53 above.

obtained *regardless* (i.e., *independently*) of the accompanying religious consequences. Indeed, there may be any number of indisputably licit public activities that eventually have a meaningful impact on an individual's religious choice: a State Department disarmament official may become so convinced of the evils of war as to decide to affiliate with a pacifist sect; federal antipoverty workers may, in the course of their efforts, become so influenced by the Roman Catholic bishops' pastoral letter on the economy, calling for "a Christian moral vision of economic justice for all,"[14] as to join the Catholic Church. As long as there is an independent secular impact (a term to be amplified below), there should be no violation of the Establishment Clause. (Of course, if any of the government regulations we have considered in this chapter were to conflict with a person's religious tenets, the burdensome effect principle would make them subject to review under the Free Exercise Clause.)

REASONS FOR INVALIDATION

Some proposals for interpreting the Religion Clauses ignore the effects of government action. For example, under the neutrality approach, as long as the state regulation does not draw a religious classification, that it favorably (or adversely) affects religious interests within a sufficiently larger category is irrelevant to its constitutionality. This also appears to be the essence of the Supreme Court's present reading of the Free Exercise Clause.[15]

Most significant efforts to develop legal doctrines for the resolution of disputes under the Establishment Clause, however, attribute substantial importance to impact. Thus a major element of the Supreme Court's famous *"Lemon"* test, the governing approach to judging Establishment Clause issues beginning in the early 1970s, is that a law's "principal or primary effect must be one that neither advances nor inhibits

14. See Leedes, 1987 Am. B. Found. Res. J. at 327–28.
15. See p. 55 above.

religion."[16] In her development of the endorsement approach, Justice O'Connor also emphasized the effect of government action by making the *perception* of a reasonable or objective observer determinative.[17] In addition, Justice Kennedy's "coercion" approach—originally constructed as an alternative to both the *Lemon* test and the endorsement proposal[18] and, in my view, the operative standard in the Supreme Court for Establishment Clause questions, at least during the 1992–93 term[19]—looks almost exclusively to the way the challenged regulation operates.[20]

Just as the burdensome effect principle requires special scrutiny for a certain kind of government action that adversely affects religious interests, so is the independent impact principle in accordance with the dominant view by making regulations vulnerable under the Establishment Clause if they produce a certain type of benefit to sectarian interests and violative of that constitutional provision if they also pose a significant threat to religious freedom. We now turn to the task of identifying this special kind of aid to religion and the reasons for holding it invalid.

MEANS AND ENDS

With the possible exception of some deliberate efforts by government to favor sectarian interests, there are virtually

16. Lemon v. Kurtzman, 403 U.S. 602, 612 (1971). The Court's earlier "test" also required that a law's "primary effect" not be either "the advancement or inhibition of religion." Abington School District v. Schempp, 374 U.S. 203, 222 (1963).

17. See p. 27 above.

18. See Jesse H. Choper, Separation of Church and State: "New" Directions by the "New" Supreme Court, 34 J. Ch. & State 363, 364–65 (1992).

19. See 61 U.S. L. Week 2240 (1993). The support of now retired Justice Byron White was, however, necessary to this conclusion. See Jesse H. Choper, Benchmarks, 79 A.B.A. J. 78, 80 (Nov. 1993). In the first Establishment Clause case in which she participated, Board of Education of Kiryas Joel Village School District v. Grumet, 114 S.Ct. 2481 (1994), the position of Justice Ruth Bader Ginsburg—Justice White's successor—appears to fulfill my earlier speculation of "her being much more a church-state separationist than Justice White." 79 A.B.A. J. at 80.

20. Allegheny County v. ACLU, 492 U.S. 573, 655 (1989) (Kennedy, J., concurring in part and dissenting in part).

no laws whose *only effect* is to aid religion; practically every government rule can reasonably be found to ultimately influence some public-welfare end. A number of such regulations, however, accomplish the secular goal only as a consequence of the prior achievement of a religious purpose; to put it another way, the secular effect depends on (derives from) the initial completion of the religious aim. These laws, in Madison's words, "employ Religion as an engine of Civil policy."[21] To immunize them because of their public-welfare benefits would, I believe, effectively read much of the core of the Establishment Clause out of the First Amendment. For example, it would justify state subsidy of that church the government found best inculcates its members with the deep convictions that make for better citizenship. This kind of government action has no *independent secular impact* and thus triggers a further inquiry that may lead to its invalidity under the independent impact principle.

EXAMPLES

Specific instances will help illustrate this important genre. It has, for example, been maintained that public school prayer recitation and Bible reading serve the secular purpose of producing profound convictions in children, thus making them better citizens.[22] But if such are the consequences, they come about only after the initial goal of these practices—the implanting of spiritual and religious beliefs—is achieved; the purported secular ends are derivative from the earlier religious effect. Similarly, it was once suggested that, as part of a state's mental health budget, funds might be granted to the Roman Catholic Church and the Protestant Episcopal Church to subsidize confession costs because of their therapeutic value.[23] But the purported mental health benefit—a

21. James Madison, Memorial and Remonstrance against Religious Assessments, ¶ 5, set forth in Everson v. Board of Education, 330 U.S. 1, 67 (1947) (app.).

22. See discussion in Jesse H. Choper, Religion in the Public Schools: A Proposed Constitutional Standard, 47 Minn. L. Rev. 329, 336 (1963).

23. Robert P. Davidow, Government Aid to Church-Affiliated Colleges: An Analysis of a Possible Answer to the Constitutional Question, 43 N.D. L. Rev. 659, 679 (1967).

concededly secular result—would come about solely as a consequence of the penitent's having obtained spiritual satisfaction; the only *independent* effect is religious. This example is analytically indistinguishable from the order of a juvenile court requiring delinquent minors to attend the church of their choice each week[24] based on the judge's belief and experience that the inculcation of religious faith will diminish the chance of recidivism. In all these cases the government programs should be held to abridge the Establishment Clause because, regardless of their purpose, they (1) have no independent secular impact and (2) pose a meaningful threat to religious liberty.

Exploration of the facts in two Supreme Court cases during the late 1980s provides informative final examples. In *Bowen v. Kendrick* the Court held that the Adolescent Family Life Act did not, "on its face," violate the Establishment Clause.[25] The federal statute granted funds to a variety of public and private agencies (including religious organizations) to provide counseling for prevention of sexual intercourse by young girls and boys. Congress's hope of reducing the social and economic costs of teenage sexual activity, pregnancy, and parenthood through promotion of "self discipline and other prudent approaches to the problem of adolescent premarital sexual relations"[26] might well be thought to be most effectively achieved by having religiously affiliated grantees teach youngsters about "fundamental elements of religious doctrine."[27] But since this concededly secular goal would be accomplished only as a consequence of the youths' first being successfully inculcated with "the views of a particular faith"[28]—an effect that, if disclosed by the record, *all* members of the Court would have found to be unconstitutional—the program would fail the independent impact principle. Regardless of Congress's good intentions, the public-

---

24. Compare Nelson v. Heyne, 355 F. Supp. 451 (N.D. Ind. 1972) with Theriault v. Carlson, 339 F. Supp. 375 (N.D. Ga. 1972).
25. 487 U.S. 589, 593 (1988).
26. 42 U.S.C. § 300z(b)(1).
27. 487 U.S. at 598.
28. Id. at 621.

welfare goal was dependent on religious indoctrination that was underwritten by the expenditure of tax funds.

The generally acknowledged prohibition on the use of public money to further religion,[29] even as a means of ultimately fulfilling a desirable secular end, was also at issue in the *Witters* case. Although the Court unanimously upheld the vocational assistance grant to a visually handicapped student at a Christian college, it would be unconstitutional under the independent impact principle. State funds were being spent for religious education: the recipient was studying to be a pastor, a missionary, or a religious youth director. I do not disagree with the likely proposition that the state's purpose was exclusively secular: training people with serious eyesight problems for productive employment. Nor would I dispute the fact that the state in no way required religious study; any promising vocational program would qualify. Nonetheless, *in Witters's case* his use of the plan employed religion as an engine of civil policy: the state's public-welfare goal (a job for the visually impaired) could be achieved as *a result of Witters's vocational education* only if he continued to work in the furtherance of his religion. In contrast, the state's secular aim in restoring the Catholic missions, discussed earlier,[30] could be fully accomplished even if the buildings were never again used for religious purposes. Nor would the *Witters* situation be affected by the fact that *ultimately* there might well be a net gain to the state treasury in that the cost of providing religious training would be exceeded by the savings of having the recipient gainfully employed instead of on the welfare rolls. That logic would validate government's paying the costs of inculcating religious beliefs in adolescents in order to relieve the much greater public expense connected with teenage pregnancy.

PRIVATE CHOICE

A major element of the Court's rationale in *Witters* was that the "principal or primary effect" of the state's program

---

29. See id. at 624 (Kennedy, J., joined by Scalia, J., concurring).
30. See at note 4 above.

did not advance religion: since the assistance is "made available generally without regard to the sectarian-nonsectarian, or public-nonpublic nature of the institution benefited, . . . any aid . . . that ultimately flows to religious institutions does so only as a result of the genuinely independent and private choices of aid recipients."[31] This "neutrality" point also played a key role in other church-state rulings of the Supreme Court during the 1980s. In *Widmar v. Vincent* the Court upheld the use by a student religious group of a state university public forum by noting that "the forum is available to a broad class of nonreligious as well as religious speakers; . . . provision of benefits to so broad a spectrum of groups is an important index of secular effect."[32] In *Board of Education v. Mergens,* when holding that a public school that maintained a "limited open forum" could allow a Christian students' club to meet on school premises during noninstructional time, the Court reasoned that "the logic of *Widmar* applies with equal force."[33] In *Mueller v. Allen,*[34] the Court sustained a state income tax deduction for expenses of parents in educating their children at elementary and secondary schools. Acknowledging that "financial assistance provided to parents ultimately has an economic effect comparable to that of aid given directly to the schools attended by their children," the Court concluded that when "public funds become available only as a result of numerous, private choices of individual parents . . . no 'imprimatur of State approval,' *Widmar,* can be deemed to have been conferred on any particular religion, or on religion generally."[35] Moreover, the Court more recently explained that "essential to our holding"[36] in its earlier landmark decision of *Walz v. Tax Commission of New York City,*[37] sustaining a state tax exemption for "real or personal prop-

31. 474 U.S. at 487.
32. 454 U.S. at 274.
33. 496 U.S. at 248.
34. 463 U.S. 388 (1983).
35. Id. at 399.
36. Texas Monthly, Inc. v. Bullock, 489 U.S. 1, 12 (1989).
37. 397 U.S. 664 (1970).

erty used exclusively for religious, educational or charitable purposes," was the fact that "the benefits derived by religious organizations flowed to a large number of nonreligious groups as well."[38]

As I discussed in chapter 1 when considering the neutrality approach, I believe the thrust of this analysis permits forms of government support for religion that subvert historical and contemporary aims of the Establishment Clause. There is no inevitable logic that drives one to this judgment, and it can be forcefully countered that "the most effective way for the modern state to disparage any institution is to deny it financial benefits to which others are entitled as a matter of course."[39] Nonetheless, I believe that the situations just described carry the possible danger of substantial, impermissible aid to sectarian causes, thereby seriously abridging religious freedom. This potential pitfall is effectively avoided if the government action has an independent secular impact, that is, an effect that itself serves the nonreligious public welfare.

As we have seen in our earlier discussion of the *Mergens* case, when a state regulation favors religious interests as part of a larger category of beneficiaries this may reasonably be made subject to the intentional advantage principle: although the conclusion is by no means indisputable, in my view as long as the process of inclusion and exclusion requires government officials to judge the group's purpose or activities, even under very broadly stated criteria, the state's according its imprimatur may fairly be viewed as "favoring" (or "endorsing") the selected group. That individuals may have *chosen* to become part of one of the beneficiary groups does not undermine the fact that an advantage has been deliberately afforded to religious interests. In *Mergens,* however, that there were a wide range of attractive alternatives to joining the Christian students' club led us to the judgment that there

38. 489 U.S. at 11.
39. Michael S. Paulsen, Religion, Equality, and the Constitution: An Equal Protection Approach to Establishment Clause Adjudication, 61 Notre Dame L. Rev. 311, 354–55 (1986).

was no meaningful threat to religious liberty and thus no violation of the Establishment Clause. We also found no constitutional violation in *Widmar* because even though the challenged practice fell under the intentional advantage principle, there was no meaningful allocation of public resources and no other significant danger to religious freedom.

The *Witters* case affords a different perspective. Even if one rejects the position that the state's approval of the Christian college as a grant recipient constitutes government action that intentionally favors religious interests, the expenditure is subject to (and fails) the independent impact test: regardless of the state's purpose, the allocation had no independent secular impact (and resulted in the use of public funds for religious training). That the Christian college benefited only along with other educational institutions, and that Witters selected it exclusively as a function of his own free will, should make no more difference than that the congressional program in *Bowen v. Kendrick* financed a broad spectrum of techniques to combat teenage pregnancy in addition to alleged religious indoctrination, and that parents' decision to send their children to the Catholic Church's lessons was the product of their private choice. On the hypothesized facts in *Bowen,* Congress was using religion as an engine of civil policy and expending tax funds for sectarian instruction. That is unconstitutional under my thesis. Similarly, unless it is shown that the financial benefit accorded religion by a tax exemption for church property is commensurate with some secular benefit from church to state—for example, "social welfare services or 'good works' that some churches perform . . . family counselling, aid to the elderly and the infirm, and to children"[40]—that public funds are subsidizing educational and charitable organizations as well as sectarian ones should not affect the outcome.[41]

One final matter: If recipients of state-provided old-age

40. Walz v. Tax Commission, 397 U.S. at 674.
41. The problem of aid to parochial schools raised in the *Mueller* case will be considered in the section that follows.

assistance donate a portion to their church or if public employees contribute a percentage of their salary to their religion, how is this "privately directed" allocation of tax funds for sectarian ends distinguishable from the cases we have been discussing? The following is my response: In the two situations just described, the government has fully accomplished the public-welfare goals sought by its allocations—providing sustenance to the elderly and obtaining labor from its staff. After this "independent secular impact" has been achieved, the welfare recipients and state workers have uninhibited free choice. They may use their money in any way they wish: spend it, save it, or give it away. Government does not condition its grant, as it did, for example, in *Witters,* on the recipient's channeling the funds to a specific, limited class of ultimate beneficiaries, which class includes church-affiliated institutions. With employee compensation and old-age assistance there is no government proviso whatever to utilize tax funds for religious purposes. But a state condition that a tuition subsidy be transferred to some qualified school (including a Christian college) is analytically identical to a state payment to any voluntary association that recipients join (including their church or synagogue). Government has thereby restricted full freedom of choice as to how tax funds will be spent. Akin to the state's approval of the use made of school premises by student groups during extracurricular periods,[42] it has singled out religion, albeit as part of a larger category, for government financial aid. If the ultimate religiously affiliated beneficiary does not render secular services in return, tax raised funds will be used for strictly religious purposes, and even though a nonreligious goal will ultimately be accomplished, it will come about only after a sectarian end is first achieved.

Concededly, the distinction between government's dispensing money to persons who have "uninhibited free choice" as to its disposition and the state's allocating funds "on condition" is not quite so clean as implied, because gov-

42. See pp. 22–23, 32–33, 149 above.

ernment imposes *some* restrictions on *all* who use money, including welfare recipients and state employees. For example, it would be unlawful for them to spend the money to buy contraband. Here again, however, the difference in degree appears to be so large as to approach being a difference in kind, one I believe is adequate to justify the distinction drawn.

AID TO PAROCHIAL SCHOOLS

The highly controversial and frequently litigated question of public financial assistance to church-related elementary and secondary schools, which lends itself to analysis under the independent impact principle, remains to be discussed.

RECORD IN THE SUPREME COURT

Almost all of the Court's rulings in this area have employed the "*Lemon*" test: "First, the statute must have a secular legislative purpose; second, its principal or primary effect must be one that neither advances nor inhibits religion; finally, the statute must not foster 'an excessive government entanglement with religion.' "[43] Beginning with the *Lemon* case itself, which involved state augmentation of salaries for teachers of secular subjects (such as mathematics, physical science, modern foreign languages, and physical education) in private schools, most decisions have invalidated the aid programs. The Court has regularly found the first prong of its test—a "secular legislative purpose"—satisfied, conceding that the state's aim had been to improve the quality of education received by children who attend nonpublic schools. In some of the cases, however, the Court has condemned the programs because they failed the second prong of its test: the aid might have the "primary effect" of advancing religion. But it has been the third prong of the test—"excessive government entanglement with religion"—that has effectively posed the greatest obstacle to state assistance to parochial schools. The Court, observing that the major beneficiaries of

43. Lemon v. Kurtzman, 403 U.S. 602, 612–13 (1971).

awards to nonpublic elementary and secondary schools are those operated by the Roman Catholic Church, has found that the mission of these (and other church-related) schools is to teach religion, and that all subjects either are, or carry the potential of being, "permeated" with sectarian thought. The Court therefore has reasoned that in order to ensure that government aid does not advance the inculcation of religious doctrine (and thus run afoul of the second prong of its test), the state would have to engage in comprehensive surveillance of the recipient schools. This would foster an impermissible degree of administrative entanglement between church and state (thus failing the third prong of the Court's test). As a consequence, a state that wished to fund parochial schools would be faced with an insoluble dilemma. Since the Court has presumed that church-related elementary and secondary schools are "permeated" with religion, it has often required that even the most neutral forms of aid (such as maps and tape recorders) be continually monitored so as to ensure that they would not be used for religious purposes; but such monitoring has engendered "excessive entanglement" and thus rendered the program invalid.

It is fair to say that application of the Court's three-part *Lemon* test has produced a conceptual disaster area, generating ad hoc judgments that are incapable of being reconciled on any principled basis. For example, a provision for therapeutic and diagnostic health services to parochial school pupils by public employees was held invalid if provided *in* the parochial school[44] but not if offered at a neutral site, even a mobile unit immediately adjacent to the parochial school.[45] Reimbursement to parochial schools for the expense of administering teacher-prepared tests required by state law was held invalid,[46] but the state could compensate parochial schools for the expense of administering state-prepared tests.[47] The government could lend textbooks to parochial

44. Meek v. Pittenger, 421 U.S. 349 (1975).
45. Wolman v. Walter, 433 U.S. 229 (1977).
46. Levitt v. Committee for Public Education, 413 U.S. 472 (1973).
47. Committee for Public Education v. Regan, 444 U.S. 646 (1980).

school pupils because, the Court explained, the books can be checked in advance for religious content and are "self-policing";[48] but the government could not lend other seemingly "self-policing" instructional items such as tape recorders, films, movie projectors, laboratory equipment, and maps.[49] The public could underwrite the cost of bus transportation to parochial schools,[50] which the Court has ruled are permeated with religion; but the public was forbidden to pay for transportation for field trips "to governmental, industrial, cultural, and scientific centers designed to enrich the secular studies of students."[51] A partial tuition tax credit to parents who sent their children to nonpublic schools (or a comparable grant for those too poor to benefit from a tax credit) was forbidden because the class of beneficiaries did not include *all* students,[52] but an income tax deduction for education expenses at nonprofit schools (public, private, or church-related) was held permissible even though 96 percent of the tuition deductions were taken by parents who sent their children to parochial schools.[53] Indeed, in an unusually candid dictum, the Court forthrightly conceded that its approach in this area "sacrifices clarity and predictability for flexibility"[54]—a euphemism for expressly admitting the absence of any principled rationale for its product.

APPLICATION OF THE THESIS

Parochial schools, virtually everyone would agree, perform a dual function, providing both religious and secular education. Since spending public funds for sectarian purposes violates the religious freedom of taxpayers, the logical thrust of the intentional advantage principle would forbid government aid to church-related schools as long as it was

48. Board of Education v. Allen, 392 U.S. 236 (1968); Meek, 421 U.S. at 365.
49. Id.
50. Everson v. Board of Education, 330 U.S. 1 (1947).
51. Wolman, 433 U.S. at 252.
52. Committee for Public Education v. Nyquist, 413 U.S. 756 (1973).
53. Mueller v. Allen, 463 U.S. 388, 401 (1983).
54. Regan, 444 U.S. at 662.

clear to the legislators that the money would inevitably be used for religious ends, that is, in support of an ideology that would be constitutionally forbidden if taught in the public schools.[55] Even the strongest advocates of government assistance for church-related schools agree that "it is just and proper for the government to refuse to pay the incremental cost of religious components of the education, in light of the conscientious objection many taxpayers have toward mandatory support for religious instruction."[56] If it could be shown, however, that the state receives full secular value for its money regardless of any benefit to religion (as in purchasing wine from the Christian Brothers), then its expenditure would have an independent secular effect. There would be no danger to religious liberty, and there would be no violation of either the intentional advantage or the independent impact principle.

Using tax funds to support the concededly secular aspects of parochial education is no different analytically from the state's judgment either to provide funds for parochial school pupils if they attended existing public schools or to establish additional public schools at various sites for all students at present attending parochial schools, neither of which would raise a colorable constitutional objection. This point is not made to urge that political fairness justifies government aid for church-related schools. Rather, it demonstrates that, when the state affords public money to finance the secular aspects of education in church-related schools (whether at the elementary, secondary, or college level), it imposes a tax burden analogous to what it could constitutionally spend for separate secular facilities. This in no way violates the historical and contemporary policy underlying the Establishment Clause against infringing religious liberty through taxation for religious purposes.

In addition, it is possible that affording some government

55. See chapter 4 above.
56. Michael W. McConnell, The Selective Funding Problem: Abortions and Religions Schools, 104 Harv. L. Rev. 989, 1018 (1991).

support to nonpublic schools (but substantially less than the per capita public school cost) would bring about a net *decrease* in the tax burden: a number of nonpublic school pupils who would otherwise shift to public schools for economic reasons might not do so and, as is sometimes predicted, many public school students might transfer to parochial or private schools. The point, however, is that this latter argument is not of constitutional import, because a net *increase* in tax burden should be equally constitutional if the state aid was limited to the secular aspects of education in parochial schools. Nor could government finance religious instruction in the hope, or even with the assurance, that this would in some way produce a smaller overall tax burden. Economically, the argument is appealing. Constitutionally, however, it would be a patent use of religion as an engine of civil policy in violation of the Establishment Clause.

Compensable Amount

We shall soon turn to the complex question of how to measure the secular educational services rendered by church-affiliated schools. Assuming that these services may be isolated, no difficulty arises where their cost is the same to the parochial school as to the public school system. Because government may properly finance the secular education of all children, whatever their religious faith, payment to a parochial school in these circumstances of the same amount that such education costs in the public schools is immune from Establishment Clause protest: no tax funds are being expended for religious purposes; no more public dollars are being used than would be if the pupils were in public schools; and the church obtains no financial benefit except compensation for the cost of secular services rendered.[57] A fortiori,

57. Public financing might well enable the church to use funds formerly spent on secular education for strictly religious purposes. This "freed funds" dynamic is produced by every concededly valid direct or indirect public aid to religiously affiliated institutions and is of no analytic consequence. For fuller treatment, see Jesse H. Choper, The Establishment Clause and Aid to Parochial Schools, 56 Calif. L. Rev. 260, 319–21 (1968).

there is no problem if the cost of providing this service in the parochial school is less than in the public school system, as is not unlikely, and government pays the parochial school only this lesser amount.

But suppose the cost of providing secular educational services in the parochial school is less than the cost for the public school system and government pays the parochial school the latter amount. Here too no more tax funds are being expended than would be if the pupils were in public schools. Even though the church obtains a net financial benefit, this should not violate the Establishment Clause. Many church-related agencies offer secular services that are funded—or purchased, if you will—by the government. If any organization—profit or nonprofit, religious or nonsectarian—provides a secular service to government at the "going rate" and is able to profit thereby because of low labor costs, greater efficiency, or any other reason, the Constitution should not be held to prohibit it.[58] In fact, for government to refuse to deal on equal terms with an organization providing such goods or services because the group is religiously affiliated would violate the Free Exercise Clause under the deliberate disadvantage principle.

Measuring Secular Value

The most complicated matter concerning public financial assistance to parochial education involves calculating the quantum of secular learning provided by church-related schools in light of the permeation issue. It has been contended that "official Catholic doctrine refuses to recognize any distinction between secular and religious teaching."[59]

58. Thus a religiously affiliated institution may be the successful bidder in a redevelopment project, satisfying a valid public purpose, and this should not violate the Establishment Clause because the institution thereby acquired valuable property at a lower price than it would have had to pay by negotiation with the private owners, who got full value for the property from the public redevelopment authority. See Ellis v. City of Grand Rapids, 257 F. Supp. 564, 569–70 (W.D. Mich. 1966); 64th St. Residences, Inc. v. City of New York, 4 N.Y.2d 268, 150 N.E.2d 396, 174 N.Y.S.2d 1 (1958).

59. Milton R. Konvitz, Separation of Church and State: The First Freedom 14 Law & Contemp. Prob. 44, 58 (1949).

Pope Pius XI and Pope Leo XIII are quoted as ordering "that every . . . subject taught, be permeated with Christian piety,"[60] as are Catholic educators, theologians, and philosophers.[61] Protestant Christian schools are said to "bathe every academic subject in scripture. . . . No dividing line exists between academics and religion because Christian schools consider the two inseparably linked."[62] A Lutheran school manual demands "that all areas of the curriculum reflect an adequate philosophy of Christian education."[63] Seventh-Day Adventists declare their "endeavor to permeate all branches of learning with a spiritual outlook."[64] After all, it is asked, "if religion is taught only one or two hours a day in church schools, what is the point of maintaining the separate parochial school system?"[65] Within the past decade the newsletter of the Association of Christian Schools International has urged that "evangelism should be a normal part of the everyday curriculum in 'God's school system.' "[66]

Under the independent impact principle, only the secular aspects of parochial school education may be publicly financed. Given the conditions just described, it is fair to ask how *any* government funds may be allocated to church-related schools. Several points must be considered in response. First, "permeation" is a word of varied and imprecise meaning. Robert F. Drinan could state "the undeniable fact that secular instruction in a Catholic school is 'permeated' by a Catholic atmosphere and Catholic attitudes"[67] yet urge that "permeation should avoid every suggestion of quasi-coercion

    60. Id.
    61. See Anson P. Stokes & Leo Pfeffer, Church and State in the United States 444 (rev. ed. 1964).
    62. Paul F. Parsons, Inside America's Christian Schools 6 (1987).
    63. Quoted in George LaNoue, Public Funds for Parochial Schools? 31 (1963).
    64. Id.
    65. Id.
    66. Parsons, Inside America's Christian Schools at 12.
    67. Robert F. Drinan, Religion, the Courts, and Public Policy 229 (1963).

or 'indoctrination.'"[68] Second, the secular courses taught in parochial schools rarely, if ever, mirror exactly the classes taught in the public schools.[69] Third, although I know of no scientific study on the extent of the permeation of sectarian teaching in secular subjects in church-operated schools, it is likely that some secular-subject classes in some parochial schools are so "permeated" that they are in reality courses of sectarian indoctrination; that some instruction is completely, bona fide secular; and that much of what is taught falls between these extremes. Fourth, to admit "an admixture of religious with secular teaching"[70] is the beginning, not the end, of the inquiry; to concede that "commingling the religious with the secular teaching does not divest the whole [course or activity] of its religious permeation and emphasis"[71] is not to conclude that no part of the course or activity may be aided with public money.

A secular-subject parochial school course (or other activity) may simultaneously serve dual, independent purposes—that is, full secular value may be obtained for the time and resources expended, and religious goals may concurrently be achieved. If this is the case, the entire course (or activity) accomplishes an isolated secular end—and may therefore be fully financed—the benefit to religion notwithstanding. On the other hand, a secular-subject parochial school course (or other activity) may partially serve both religious and secular ends. Here an allocation must be made; only the secular product may be publicly financed. Of course, if a secular-subject parochial school course (or other activity) is in reality religious instruction or training, it cannot be publicly funded at all; conversely, if it is exclusively secular in effect, it may be totally funded.

One relatively effortless means of avoiding the sensitive

68. Robert F. Drinan, The Challenge to Catholic Educators in the Maryland College Case, Nat'l Catholic Educ. Ass'n Bull., May 1967, 3, 7.
69. See Choper, 56 Calif. L. Rev. at 292–94.
70. Everson, 330 U.S. at 47 (Rutledge, J., dissenting).
71. Id.

task of measurement—of finessing the need for government to define what is religious teaching and what is not (that is, as earlier observed, the same as determining what may and may not be taught in the public schools)—would be to use standardized tests to decide whether the students who attend church-related schools receive as full a secular education as students in public schools. It has recently been reported that "the best available social science evidence confirms that private religious schools are at least as effective as public secular schools under these objective standards."[72] But this method has substantial shortcomings as an accurate gauge. Apart from general problems of imprecision, the primary difficulty seems to be that achievement tests (and sociological studies) are not sufficiently comprehensive in terms of either breadth or depth to evaluate all that is taught in any school. Since they cannot ensure that the educational services rendered in parochial schools are as complete and effective as those in the public schools, or have the same impact from a nonreligious perspective on the overall development of the student, there is a real risk that state funds will be used to subsidize religious instruction or indoctrination.

Because I know of no perfect (or even highly effective) process for assessing the quantity of nonsectarian education afforded by church-related schools, I would favor using time spent as the basic criterion. This would involve courts in the unwelcome task of "separating the secular from the religious in education [which] is one of magnitude, intricacy and delicacy."[73] But just as courts, when called on to do so, must

72. McConnell, 104 Harv. L. Rev. at 989, 1004, citing James S. Coleman, Thomas Hoffer, & Sally Kilgore, High School Achievement: Public, Catholic, and Private Schools Compared 122–78 (1982) (summarizing research data). See also James S. Coleman & Thomas Hoffer, Public and Private High Schools: The Impact of Communities 63–95 (1987) (comparing academic achievement of students in public, non-Catholic private, and Catholic private schools); Andrew M. Greeley & Peter H. Rossi, The Education of Catholic Americans (1966) (comparing graduates of Catholic parochial schools with other Catholics).

73. McCollum v. Board of Education, 333 U.S. 203, 237 (1948) (Jackson, J., concurring).

determine whether a public school textbook is religiously indoctrinational, or whether a public school history course is really religious instruction, they may make the same constitutional judgment in respect to parochial school affairs. When a public school action is found to be religious, the court must enjoin it; when a parochial school practice is held to be religious, the court must forbid its public subsidy.

The ultimate judgment on the amount of permissible aid under a time-spent criterion may be reached in several ways. One method would compare the number of hours of secular teaching in the parochial school with the total hours of instruction in the jurisdiction's public schools and pay the parochial school no more than that fraction of the per capita student cost in the public schools. This would tend to shortchange parochial schools that were more efficient than the public schools and overpay those that were less productive. Another means would be to compare the number of hours of secular teaching in the parochial school with its total hours of instruction and pay it no more than that fraction of its overall costs. Other variations are also possible. Obviously, if the amount of state funding is relatively small, the need for detailed review of these issues will arise only infrequently, since the total amount of public aid will be less than the conceded value of the secular educational services rendered by the parochial school. In any event, the prohibition against the use of compulsorily raised tax funds for religious purposes, central to the concept of nonestablishment as an important guarantor of religious liberty, suggests that the state or federal financing agency and the recipient parochial school should have the burden of justifying allocation of the cost of a colorably challenged program to the secular side of the ledger. In cases of uncertainty, the issue should be resolved against the public funding.

Examples

With these points in mind, specific illustrations of problems that could arise may be helpful. The arithmetic text assigned in a Catholic elementary school might use sectarian characters, illustrations, or examples, phrasing arithmetic problems in terms of rosary beads instead of apples[74] and using pictures of parochial schools instead of public schools. Or if the text is "clean," the teacher might use these illustrations. Trumpet instruction might involve an unusual amount of religiously oriented music, and French language instruction might include a high concentration of religiously significant words or readings. It seems to me that in all these cases full secular value has been obtained for the time and resources expended, despite the fact that religious interests may also have been served.

In a parochial school biology text or course, after a full explanation of the theory of evolution, the church's perspective on the matter might also be fully articulated. Or in the civics class, the concept of racial equality might be amplified by presenting the relevant secular and also theological sources. Despite the concurrent religious educational value, and despite the fact that these matters might never be mentioned in the average public school setting, they might still have significant secular educational value. Even a parochial school course in "religion" itself might so qualify *if properly handled.*

There is a very fine line, however, between objective presentation and subtle commitment,[75] and this truth is not confined to parochial schools. Undoubtedly some texts used in public schools—and undoubtedly some teachers—intentionally or unintentionally emphasize humanistic or antireligious values. Surely the opposite is also true. Such emphasis will vary among public schools, depending in part on the cultural and religious composition of the students and

74. One math problem in a Protestant Christian school reads: "Kimberly received $10.00 for her birthday. She gave $1.50 to Sunday School, spent $3.98 on a new purse and put the rest in her savings account. How much did she put in her savings account?" Parsons, Inside America's Christian Schools at 5.

75. "It is too much to expect that mortals will teach subjects about which their contemporaries have passionate controversies with the detachment they may summon to teaching about remote subjects." McCollum v. Board of Education, 333 U.S. at 236 (Jackson, J., concurring).

teachers. To the extent that this is constitutionally permissible, effectively unavoidable, or de minimis in the public schools, it should be similarly unobjectionable in the parochial schools for the purpose of public funding—subject always to the burden of justification discussed above.

A parochial school history course or text might teach that all major events are related to or produced by one of the basic truths of the religion[76] or might emphasize the contribution of one faith over all others.[77] Parochial school texts in English composition might "stress Catholic [or Protestant] religious words and teachings,"[78] or a current events class might use a weekly magazine whose articles are "Catholic-oriented."[79] An advanced biology text or course in a fundamentalist Christian school might omit all references to birth control, sterilization, and euthanasia or specifically reject most parts of evolutionary theory and shift scientific concepts so that they appear to be based on sectarian tenets.[80] A parochial school geography book might describe only devout

76. According to one Christian school teacher in California, "in history, we say nothing happens without God's permission. History is dictated by God." Parsons, Inside America's Christian Schools at 169. The publisher of a fundamentalist Christian history text observes, "The cross of Christ is the focal point of human history." The text explains ongoing tensions in the Middle East in the following way: "The Middle East has remained the critical area of the world not only because of its vast oil resources, but also because Israel is the focal point of God's plan for the last days." Id. at 48, 51.

77. One Christian literature textbook opined that "it is a great tragedy that as talented a man as Mark Twain could never find peace with God instead of fighting Him." Id. at 40.

78. See Catholic School J., Jan. 1963, at 86 (advertisement). Some fundamentalist Christian schools use *The Christian Student Dictionary*, which injects Christian doctrine and perspective into the definitions of words. One definition of "liberal" in this dictionary is: "One who does not believe that the Bible is the inspired Word of God." Parsons, Inside America's Christian Schools at 45.

79. See Catholic School J. at 88.

80. According to one Christian biology textbook: "Some scientists say that the reptiles lived first and mammals came later. . . . From the Bible, we know that they were all created about 6,000 years ago." Parsons, Inside America's Christian Schools at 89. One textbook publisher declared that "the people who have prepared this book have tried consistently to put the word of God first and science second." Id.

Christian families in various cultures or may explain sociological events from a fundamentalist perspective;[81] the teacher
might ask the students to map all Catholic or Baptist churches
in the state.

Clearly, some of these activities cannot be fully supported
with public funds under the independent impact principle.
Either the quantity of religious perspective has deprived the
course of full secular educational value, or the quality of sectarian permeation has so slanted the material as to partially
undermine or even fully destroy its secular content. The very
description of these courses and texts states a case sufficient
to shift the burden of justifying any quantum of secular value
to those defending government support.

Vouchers

The Court has yet to formally address the constitutional
challenge to a voucher system for elementary and secondary
education, the argument being that their use in church-
related schools violates the Establishment Clause. As I have
already indicated in our discussion of the *Witters* case—which
I believe effectively resolves the constitutional question in favor of vouchers[82]—if the public subsidy exceeds the value of
the secular educational service rendered, tax funds are being
utilized for religious purposes contrary to the independent
impact principle. Furthermore, state money might be used
for religion even if the per capita amount given was equal to
or even less than the sum expended on every child in public
schools, because there is no guarantee that the parochial
school offers the same quantum of secular education as the
public schools or that the lesser amount offered costs the
parochial school as much as the sum made available to it. It

81. One textbook, in describing the Canadian Indians, opines that "because they were removed from Christian influences and their tribal customs,
many had a hard time adjusting to modern living." Id. at 47.

82. See Jesse H. Choper, The Establishment Clause and Aid to Parochial Schools—An Update, 75 Calif. L. Rev. 5, 12–14 (1987); Jesse H.
Choper, Are School Voucher Plans Constitutional? 13 Calif. Law. 35 (Oct.
1993).

follows that the religious use of tax funds could result even if the amount given is only part of the parochial school tuition, which is itself considerably less than the parochial school's cost, because even this smaller government subsidy might exceed the cost or value of the secular educational services rendered.

For similar reasons, as with the program in *Witters*, certain provisions of the World War II "GI Bill of Rights"[83] violate the independent impact principle. Under that law, as reportedly administered, the government paid tuition directly to the veteran's school, even if it was a theological seminary.[84] This was not a case in which "GI's are paid a certain amount which they can use in any way they want . . . [as] compensation for their serving in the armed forces."[85] That would be like the salaries of public employees or old-age assistance, discussed earlier. The GI Bill, however, was a case of "state conditioned" benefits, within a fairly limited category, as described above. Moreover, it is irrelevant that study at theological seminaries is "education they would have undertaken had they not been taken in the Army."[86] On this theory the government could make contributions to any voluntary association to which veterans had belonged because they would have done so had they been at home. The GI Bill would be no different from a state grant of funds to a parochial school with a proviso that it be spent for any of a designated series of programs that included sectarian teaching. Indeed, this

83. Serviceman's Readjustment Act of 1944, 58 Stat. 287.

84. Secretary of Health, Education, and Welfare, Federal Programs under Which Institutions with Religious Affiliation Receive Federal Funds through Grants or Loans, March 28, 1961 (memorandum), in S. Doc. no. 29, 87th Cong., 1st sess. 37, 44 (1961). Virgil C. Blum, Academic Freedom and Tax Support for Independent Education, 40 Phi Delta Kappan 349, 352 (1959), reports that "approximately 36,000 veterans used federal money to pay for training as Protestant ministers."

85. Comment of Leo Pfeffer, in Religion and Freedom 13 (report by David McDonald on a seminar sponsored by the Fund for the Republic, New York, N.Y., May 5–9, 1958).

86. 2 Hearings on H.R. 2361 and 2362 before the General Subcomm. on Education of the House Comm. on Education and Labor, 89th Cong., 1st sess. 1614 (1965).

closely resembles the state's providing a deaf student in a parochial school with a sign-language interpreter whose duties include communicating "the material covered in religion class, the nominally secular subjects that are taught from a religious perspective, and the daily Masses."[87] Although this last program was recently upheld by the Supreme Court, in all these situations the independent impact principle would prevent the government from channeling money to religious ends and thereby placing its imprimatur on a violation of the Religion Clauses.

87. Zobrest v. Catalina Foothills School District, 113 S.Ct. 2462, 2472 (1993) (Blackmun, J., dissenting).

Afterword: A Professional Note

A critical reviewer of the manuscript concluded that this book's thesis would be "unacceptable to every existing interest group—those who are religious, those who are hostile to religion, those who are committed to civil liberties, those who are committed to judicial restraint." Although chastened by this judgment, I did not find it surprising because I know of no one—including me—who does not disagree with some, if not many, of the results my approach produces.

On the one hand, my personal preferences are generally in accord with almost all of the outcomes I would reach under the Establishment Clause, proscribing many religious influences in the public schools but allowing substantial aid to parochial schools. Moreover, I strongly favor the protection for minority religions that I have urged under the Free Exercise Clause, a shelter not only greater than that afforded by the rule of the *Smith* case but also sturdier, in my view, than during the pre-*Smith* regime.

On the other hand, I would feel much more comfortable had I been able to develop a set of principles that interprets the Religion Clauses to prohibit school boards from excising the study of evolution from the curriculum, to prevent local governments from erecting sectarian displays on public property, and most certainly to forbid an official pronouncement that "Christianity is our religion."[1] Similarly, I believe it would be desirable if my thesis's general restriction on most forms of government financial assistance to religion were flexible enough at least to permit (if not require) exemptions

1. See pp. 157–58 above.

of the kind ordered in *Sherbert v. Verner* and approved in *Walz v. Tax Commission*.[2] Nor have I hesitated to note my wish for a broader definition than the one accorded to religious beliefs that will benefit from the special protection of the Free Exercise Clause.

After extensive reflection spanning a period of more than thirty years, however, I could find no analytically satisfactory way to accomplish these ends and still remain true to my conception of the proper role of the Supreme Court in exercising its momentous power of judicial review. On balance, then, I am willing to—and must—accept the consequences of my principles.

2. I should emphasize the real possibility that, as I once argued in an amicus brief on behalf of the United States Catholic Conference in the *Walz* case, most tax exemptions for church property may be valid under the independent impact principle because their worth may be shown to be commensurate with some secular value provided to the state by the recipient churches, see p. 172 above. For example, they might well "contribute to the well-being of the community in a variety of nonreligious ways, and thereby bear burdens that would otherwise either have to be met by general taxation, or be left undone." Walz v. Tax Commission, 397 U.S. 664, 687 (1970) (Brennan, J., concurring).

TABLE OF CASES

Names of cases cited or discussed in the text are in italics, as are the page numbers where the citation or discussion occurs.

INDEX